Living with Disability

ISSUES

Independence

Educational Publishers

Cambridge

First published by Independence

The Studio, High Green

Great Shelford

Cambridge CB22 5EG

England

© Independence 2010

Photocopy licence

The material in this book is protected by copyright. However, the
purchaser is free to make multiple copies of particular articles for instructional
purposes for immediate use within the purchasing institution.
Making copies of the entire book is not permitted.

British Library Cataloguing in Publication Data

Living with disability. -- (Issues ; v. 197)

1. People with disabilities--Legal status, laws, etc.--

Great Britain. 2. People with disabilities--Services for--

Great Britain.

I. Series II. Firth, Lisa.

362.4'0941-dc22

ISBN-13: 978 1 86168 557 5

Printed in Great Britain

MWL Print Group Ltd

CONTENTS

Chapter 1 Disability Issues

Chapter 2 Rights and Discrimination

OTHER TITLES IN THE ISSUES SERIES

For more on these titles, visit: www.independence.co.uk

EXPLORING THE ISSUES

Photocopiable study guides to accompany the above publications. Each four-page A4 guide provides a variety of discussion points and other activities to suit a wide range of ability levels and interests.

A note on critical evaluation

Because the information reprinted here is from a number of different sources, readers should bear in mind the origin of the text and whether the source is likely to have a particular bias when presenting information (just as they would if undertaking their own research). It is hoped that, as you read about the many aspects of the issues explored in this book, you will critically evaluate the information presented. It is important that you decide whether you are being presented with facts or opinions. Does the writer give a biased or an unbiased report? If an opinion is being expressed, do you agree with the writer?

Living with Disability offers a useful starting point for those who need convenient access to information about the many issues involved. However, it is only a starting point. Following each article is a URL to the relevant organisation's website, which you may wish to visit for further information.

What is disability?

There are rules about what the law counts as a disability, when considering whether or not discrimination has taken place.

The law says that 'disability' means a physical or mental impairment, which has a substantial and long-term negative effect on your ability to carry out normal day-to-day activities. There are special rules for people with cancer, HIV and multiple sclerosis and for people who are blind or partially sighted – see below.

According to this definition, impairments can include sensory impairments, such as sight and hearing, or mental impairments such as learning disabilities, dyslexia and mental illness. Some severe disfigurements count as a disability. Some conditions that can worsen over time such as multiple sclerosis and HIV/AIDS are regarded as a disability as soon as they are diagnosed, even before they start to affect your day-to-day activities.

> **The law says that 'disability' means a physical or mental impairment, which has a substantial and long-term negative effect on your ability to carry out normal day-to-day activities**

To have a long-term disability means that the disability:

⇨ has lasted for at least 12 months; or

⇨ is expected to last for at least 12 months; or

⇨ is likely to last for the rest of your life, if you are expected to live for less than 12 months.

An impairment will be treated as affecting your ability to carry out normal day-to-day activities if it affects at least one of the following:

⇨ mobility.

⇨ ability to use hands, for example, for writing or cooking.

⇨ physical co-ordination.

⇨ continence (the ability to control your bladder or bowels).

⇨ the ability to lift, carry or move ordinary objects.

⇨ speech, hearing or eyesight.

⇨ memory, or the ability to concentrate, learn or understand.

⇨ being able to recognise physical danger.

In some cases, even if medical aids or treatment are used to help control or remove a disability, it is still regarded as a disability. Examples of this include the use of an artificial limb or medication to control epilepsy. However, visual impairment corrected with glasses or contact lenses is not regarded as a disability.

Although a minor impairment may not, on its own, count as substantial, you may have a number of minor impairments which taken together may be seen as having a substantial effect. If an impairment stops having a substantial effect, it can still be regarded as an impairment if there is a reasonable likelihood of the condition recurring, for example, epilepsy.

People with cancer, HIV or multiple sclerosis

In England, Wales and Scotland, if you have cancer, HIV or multiple sclerosis, you are automatically counted as having a disability. This means that you don't have to show that you have an impairment that has a substantial, adverse, long-term effect on the ability to carry out normal day-to-day activities. You are counted as having a disability from the date you are diagnosed with the condition.

People who are blind or partially sighted

In England, Wales and Scotland, you are counted as having a disability if you are either:

⇨ certified as blind or partially-sighted by a consultant ophthalmologist; or

⇨ registered as blind or partially-sighted by a local authority.

What does not count as a disability

The law does not currently count the following as disabilities:

⇨ addiction to alcohol, nicotine or any other substance not prescribed by a doctor. However, damage to health caused by the addiction may be considered a disability.

⇨ hay fever.

⇨ certain personality disorders (e.g. exhibitionism, voyeurism or a tendency to steal, set fires, or physically or sexually abuse other people).

⇨ tattoos and body piercing.

For more information about what counts as a disability, visit the website of the Equality and Human Rights Commission at: www.equalityhumanrights.com.

If you need more information about what is a mental or physical impairment, you should consult an experienced adviser, e.g. at a Citizens Advice Bureau.

⇨ The above information is reprinted by kind permission of Citizens Advice. Visit their Adviceguide website at www.adviceguide.org.uk for more information on this and other related topics.

© Citizens Advice. Citizens Advice is an operating name of the National Association of Citizens Advice Bureaux

The Medical and Social Models of Disability

Information from Get a Plan.

The Social Model of Disability was developed in the UK in the 1960s and 1970s by the emerging Disability Movement, and in turn inspired a number of campaigns for civil rights for disabled people in the 1980s and 1990s. These years of campaigning for civil rights legislation led to the creation of the DDA in 1995, which has implications for arts organisations in the way that they respond to disabled people.

The Medical Model of Disability is still the most commonly recognised. It says that what is significant about someone is their medical history, their medical condition, what is wrong with them. The technical description of what is wrong with someone is used to determine:

⇨ what they can and cannot do;

⇨ what they will continue to be able and unable to do;

⇨ what they need.

The responsibility for managing that condition and any arising implications rests with the individual themselves. They can gain support from society to do so, but the model creates a culture of charity, since society can choose to support that disabled person or not. Any additional support they do get is provided because they are 'different' to the norm.

The Social Model of Disability instead distinguishes between someone's impairment, which is their medical condition, and the disabling barriers that they face in trying to participate in the world at large. It places the responsibility for disability on society and the environments it creates, rather than on the disabled people themselves.

A disability, according to this model, is not a medical condition, it is the stigma, oppression and stereotyping a disabled person experiences as other people encounter them, make assumptions about them and refuse to alter their own attitudes and practices to include them in their standard thinking.

These barriers might be the steps into a building, the reliance on reading written communication, or the incorrect assumptions people make about disabled people. The responsibility for removing these barriers lies with the people and organisations that create them, and those who maintain them by not challenging the status quo.

The Disability Discrimination Act supports the idea that it is the duty of society to remove, or avoid, these barriers.

More models

The Medical and the Social Models are just that – models. They are useful in specific contexts to look at how we choose to see the world. And there are many other ways of looking at disability too.

With a little Googling you might come across the Charity Model, the Affirmative Model, the Human Rights Model and the Cultural Model to name just a few.

⇨ The above information is reprinted with kind permission from Get a Plan. Visit www.getaplan.org.uk for more information.

© Get a Plan

Physical disability

Information from Children, Youth and Women's Health Service.

In the early years, children may have some difficulties in learning to move skilfully. This is not unusual. However, for some children, the muscles and nerves that control body movements may not be properly formed or may become damaged, causing a physical disability. There are organisations and services that can help you and your child if your child has a physical disability.

What is a physical disability?

A physical disability is any condition that permanently prevents normal body movement and/or control. There are many different types of physical disabilities. Some of the main ones include:

Muscular dystrophies

When a child has muscular dystrophy, this means that the muscle fibres in the body gradually weaken over time. Children can have different types of muscular dystrophy. The most common type is Duchenne Muscular Dystrophy which occurs only in boys. All types of muscular dystrophy are genetic even though other family members may not have the condition.

Acquired brain and spinal injuries

Physical disabilities may result from permanent injuries to the brain, spinal cord or limbs that prevent proper movement in parts of the body.

Spina bifida

Sometimes, a baby's spinal cord (the nerves that run down the spine) do not develop normally during pregnancy. When this happens, the child can have a physical disability called spina bifida. The type and amount of disability caused by spina bifida will depend upon the level of the abnormality of the spinal cord. Children with spina bifida may have:

⇨ partial or full paralysis of the legs;

⇨ difficulties with bowel and bladder control.

They may also have:

⇨ hydrocephalus (high pressure on the brain because of fluid not being drained away as normal);

⇨ bone and joint deformities (they may not grow normally);

⇨ curvature (bending) of the spine.

> *A physical disability is any condition that permanently prevents normal body movement and/or control. There are many different types of physical disabilities*

Cerebral palsy

Cerebral palsy is caused by damage to the parts of the brain which control movement during the early stages of development. In most cases, this damage occurs during pregnancy. However, damage can sometimes occur during birth and from brain injuries in early infancy (such as lack of oxygen from near drowning, meningitis, head injury or being shaken).

Children with cerebral palsy may have difficulties with:

⇨ posture (the ability to put the body in a chosen position and keep it there);

⇨ movement of body parts or the whole body;

- muscle weakness or tightness;
- involuntary muscle movements (spasms);
- balance and coordination;
- talking and eating.

Children can have different types of cerebral palsy:

- hemiplegia (involves muscle movements and weakness on one side of the body).
- diplegia (involves muscle movements and weakness in the lower part of the body).
- quadriplegia (involves muscle movements and weakness in both arms and both legs).
- ataxia (involves problems with balance and coordination).

There is much more about cerebral palsy in the booklet *Cerebral Palsy – an information guide for parents* written for the Royal Children's Hospital (Victoria, Australia).

http://www.rch.org.au/emplibrary/cdr/CPBooklet.pdf

Multiple disabilities

Some children with physical disabilities will have other disabilities, such as intellectual, visual or hearing impairments. They may also have communication difficulties or other medical conditions such as epilepsy or asthma. When a child has several different types of disability, professionals talk about multiple disabilities rather than listing separate conditions.

Causes of physical disabilities

There are many different causes of physical disabilities. These include:

- inherited or genetic disorders, such as muscular dystrophy;
- conditions present at birth (congenital), such as spina bifida;
- serious illness affecting the brain, nerves or muscles, such as meningitis;
- spinal cord injury;
- brain injury.

Role of a physiotherapist

Physiotherapists can help children with disabilities and their families by:

- assisting the child to learn how to use parts of the body and develop physical skills;
- helping a child to become mobile (either independently or by using equipment);
- helping parents to become skilful in assisting their

child, including lifting, positioning and physical care;
- working with staff from the child's preschool or school.

Role of an occupational therapist

Occupational therapists are often called OTs. The role of an OT is to help a child become fully involved in all aspects of life – at home, at preschool or school and within the general community.

OTs work with each child in different ways depending upon the child's disability, interests and skills. For example, an OT may give advice on any physical changes needed in the home or the child's preschool or school. This advice can include information on the type of stairs, handrail or ramp that will be best for the child. An OT may suggest changes to toys, equipment or furniture and can also advise on ways to improve writing and other hand skills.

Role of a speech pathologist

Children with a physical disability may need help with talking. Some will learn to use alternative methods of communication such as:

- communication boards or charts;
- electronic devices;
- sign language.

A speech pathologist will assess a child's ability to understand and express thoughts, feelings and ideas, and help to improve communication skills using speech or alternatives to speech. A speech pathologist can also help with eating and drinking problems.

Other important professionals

A number of other health professionals may be involved in helping your child. These include the:

- orthopaedic surgeon who examines a child's muscles and/or bone structure and provides surgery to manage problems related to these;
- ophthalmologist who is a specialist eye and vision doctor;
- paediatric rehabilitation specialist who assesses and manages the physical condition of children and young people with chronic (ever-present) disabilities;
- orthotist who provides corrective equipment such as splints;
- psychologist who assesses cognitive (thinking) skills and helps to manage emotional and behavioural problems;
- audiologist who assesses hearing.

Special equipment

Many different professionals and agencies can provide advice about equipment for children with physical disabilities. Which will be the best source of information depends upon the needs of your child and your family.

Depending upon your problems, you may need to speak with a physiotherapist, speech pathologist or an occupational therapist. Each of these therapists knows enough about the work of the others to be able to advise you about who could be most useful.

At different times, your child may require equipment to help with:

⇨ walking/mobility;

⇨ talking/communication;

⇨ eating;

⇨ toileting;

⇨ showering/bathing.

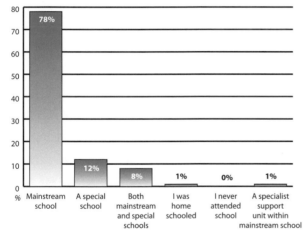

Type of school attended

More than three-quarters of respondents who became disabled before completing their formal education attended a mainstream school.

78%	Mainstream school	
12%	A special school	
8%	Both mainstream and special schools	
1%	I was home schooled	
0%	I never attended school	
1%	A specialist support unit within mainstream school	

Discrimination at school, college or university

54% of respondents who had been disabled before completing their formal education had experienced discrimination or prejudice at school, college or university. The breakdown of this discrimination by institution is as follows:

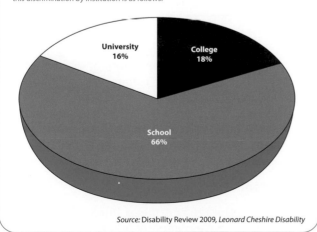

University 16%

College 18%

School 66%

Source: Disability Review 2009, Leonard Cheshire Disability

Some equipment for children with physical disabilities can include computer and electronic technology, especially for assistance with communication.

What you can do

⇨ In some families, physical disabilities can be inherited. If your child has an inherited condition such as muscular dystrophy, you may wish to speak to a genetic counsellor. A genetic counsellor will study your family history and explain the risks of any inherited condition being passed to other children. This counsellor would also be able to provide information to you when you are planning to have children if someone in your family has had an inherited disability. Speak to your family doctor or contact your local hospital for further information.

⇨ A healthy diet before and during pregnancy can help to prevent some physical disabilities. In particular, extra folate before and around the time of becoming pregnant help to prevent spina bifida.

⇨ Immunisation against serious childhood illness will help to prevent some physical disabilities.

⇨ Prevent serious injury to the child's brain or spine through, for example, car and home safety.

If your child has a physical disability:

⇨ Where possible, enrol at child care, preschool or school well before your child is due to attend so that necessary changes to stairs, toilets or classrooms can be completed.

⇨ Help teachers by giving them up-to-date information about your child's medical and physical needs. This will assist teachers in choosing the best teaching methods for your child.

Preschool and school

At preschool or school, teachers will discuss physical changes, special equipment and support needs for your child. Sometimes, teachers may be able to get extra help in the classroom or advice from visiting specialist teachers.

Preschools and schools may need to apply for grants to make changes to classrooms and buildings, such as installing wheelchair access ramps or special toilets. Expensive or complex changes to the site may take some time to complete.

⇨ The above information is reprinted with kind permission from the Children, Youth and Women's Health Service in Australia. Visit www.cyh.com for more.

CHILDREN, YOUTH AND WOMEN'S HEALTH SERVICE

Learning disabilities

Information from British Institute of Learning Disabilities.

Summary

⇨ 'Learning disability' is a label which is convenient for certain purposes, but people with learning disabilities are always people first.

⇨ Different ways of defining and classifying learning disability are used, but all are open to some interpretation.

⇨ There are few official statistics for numbers of people with a learning disability, and our knowledge is based on studies of prevalence.

⇨ The causes of learning disabilities are not fully classified, but are mainly environmental or genetic factors, or chromosomal abnormalities.

⇨ Support for people with learning disabilities has moved away from the medical model to a social model based on inclusion and integration.

Terminology

The term 'learning disability' is a label. It is convenient in discussion and for planning services. But people who carry that label wear many others, such as friend, neighbour, relative, employee, colleague, fellow citizen. A label describes one aspect of a person, but does not capture the whole person. Many people with learning disabilities prefer the term learning difficulties. This is the wording used by People First, an international advocacy organisation. In the UK, the Warnock Committee has suggested that learning difficulties should be used to refer to specific problems with learning in children that might arise as a result of issues such as medical problems, emotional problems, and language impairments. Learning disabilities can be a useful term in that it indicates an overall impairment of intellect and function. Alternative expressions are also used, for example developmental disabilities and intellectual disabilities. There is at present no clear consensus. It is, however, widely accepted that whatever terms are used they should be clear, inclusive and positive.

Definitions

The World Health Organization defines learning disabilities as:

'a state of arrested or incomplete development of mind'.

Learning disability is a diagnosis, but it is not a disease, nor is it a physical or mental illness. Unlike the latter,

so far as we know it is not treatable. Internationally three criteria are regarded as requiring to be met before learning disabilities can be identified:

⇨ Intellectual impairment

⇨ Social or adaptive dysfunction

⇨ Early onset

Intellectual impairment

IQ is one way of classifying learning disability:

⇨ **50-70** mild learning disability

⇨ **35-50** moderate learning disability

⇨ **20-35** severe learning disability

⇨ **below 20** profound learning disability

However, there are problems with using IQ alone. Measurements can vary during a person's growth and development. Also, many of us have individual strengths and abilities which do not show up well in IQ tests. It is important to take into account as well the degree of social functioning and adaptation.

> ### The World Health Organization defines learning disabilities as 'a state of arrested or incomplete development of mind'

Social or adaptive dysfunction

Measuring the degree of impairment of social functioning can be difficult, too. Clearly, some social impairments may be life threatening for the person, for example poor skills in eating and drinking, and in keeping warm and safe. Others, such as communication and social abilities, may be important to the individual's functioning in modern society. Also relevant are the extent of difficulties with understanding, learning and remembering new things, and in generalising any learning to new situations. Assessments of functioning should take into account the context within which the person is living, including personal and family circumstances, age, gender, culture and religion.

Early onset

The third criterion is that these impairments can be identified in the developmental period of life. They are

present from childhood, not acquired later as a result of an accident, adult disease or illness, or dementia.

Other definitions

Within mental health legislation, the criminal justice system, and in relation to social security benefits, other terms and criteria may be used. It is important to recognise that these exist for specific legal purposes. This means that someone who fits the definition for one piece of legislation may not be covered by another.

Classifications

All levels of learning disability are points on a spectrum, and there are no clear dividing lines between them, or between people with mild learning disabilities and the general population. Some individuals with mild learning disabilities may even not be diagnosed because they function and adapt well socially. Most can communicate using spoken language, have reasonable skills, and given the chance can manage well with lower-level but appropriate support. People with moderate to profound learning disabilities need a good deal more care and support. This frequently includes special help with communication, a higher degree of risk assessment and protection, and more physical help with mobility, continence and eating.

All levels of learning disability are points on a spectrum, and there are no clear dividing lines between them

Numbers

Just as there is no consensus on terminology, there are no official statistics that tell us precisely how many people there are with learning disabilities in the UK. The information we have comes from a number of population studies which have focused on measuring prevalence rates. On a statistical basis 2.5% of the population should have learning disabilities. In fact, prevalence seems to be lower at about 1-2%, giving a total of between 602,000 and 1,204,000 in a UK population of 60.2 million. Partly this is because mortality is higher among people with more severe forms of learning disability than in the general population. Also, in part it is due to not all cases of mild learning disabilities being identified. We can be more accurate about the numbers of people with moderate to profound learning disabilities because they almost all use services of some kind. They are thought to represent 0.35% of the total UK population, or about 210,700 people.

Causes

There are a number of reasons for finding out where possible the cause of a person's learning disabilities. One is that often individuals and their families want to know, and have a right to do so. There are also health factors. It is important to distinguish between learning disability and physical or mental health problems which may well be treatable. In addition, some forms of learning disability or syndromes are indicative of the likelihood of certain health problems occurring. Genetic counselling may also be needed for the family, and increasingly for people with learning disabilities themselves who plan to become parents. Among people who have a mild learning disability, in about 50% of cases no cause has been identified. A number of environmental and genetic factors are thought to be significant, although clearly diagnosed genetic causes have been found in only 5% of people in this category. Higher rates in some social classes suggest that factors such as large families, overcrowding and poverty are important. Research increasingly points also to organic causes, such as exposure to alcohol and other toxins prior to birth, hypoxia and other problems at the time of birth, and some chromosomal abnormalities. In people with severe or profound learning disabilities, chromosomal abnormalities cause about 40% of cases. Genetic factors account for 15%, prenatal and perinatal problems 10%, and postnatal issues a further 10%. Cases which are of unknown cause are fewer, but still high at around 25%.

Support

With the decline of the medical model of learning disabilities, the focus of support has shifted to health and social care, and to education. At the same time, the training of professionals and support staff in these areas is improving in content and structure. As a result, people with learning disabilities are beginning to lead longer and better quality lives. Emphasis is now on inclusive approaches and community integration. Direct payments to enable individuals to purchase their own services, together with the growth of advocacy, are giving greater choice and control to people with learning disabilities in running their own lives. Developments in person-centred approaches and independent supported living are changing expectations. The combined effect is that new opportunities are being opened up for people with learning disabilities in areas such as employment, parenthood, lifelong learning and citizenship. Even so, much remains to be done.

⇨ The above information is reprinted with kind permission from the British Institute of Learning Disabilities. Visit www.bild.org.uk for more information.

© British Institute of Learning Disabilities

BRITISH INSTITUTE OF LEARNING DISABILITIES

Hidden disabilities

Information from the NUS.

The NUS SWD (Students With Disabilities) Campaign is committed to campaigning and fighting for equal human and civil rights for all students with disabilities. Yet not all disabilities are obvious. Part of the NUS SWD Campaign is focused upon raising awareness and campaigning for hidden disabilities. Hidden or invisible disabilities are physical or mental impairments that are not readily apparent to others. Around 70% of people who have a disability in this country have a hidden disability. This article will give you an idea of different hidden disabilities, ways to campaign and organisations you can work with.

Types of hidden disabilities

These are just a few:

⇨ Asthma: More than three million people have asthma in the UK.

⇨ Mental ill health: It is estimated that one in four people will experience mental ill health.

⇨ Epilepsy: one in 200 people in the UK has epilepsy. It is a neurological condition characterised by seizures that happen when the electrical system of the brain malfunctions.

⇨ Diabetes: The number of people with diabetes is increasing. Diabetes is an illness which occurs as a result of problems with the production and supply of insulin in the body.

⇨ Autism: Autistic spectrum disorders are estimated to touch the lives of over 500,000 families throughout the UK.

⇨ Arthritis: An estimated eight million people have arthritis in the UK.

⇨ Myalgic Encephalomyelitis (ME): People with ME may tire more quickly than other people and in more serious cases the sense of balance and co-ordination may be affected to varying degrees.

⇨ Dyslexia: The BDA estimates that four per cent of the UK population is severely dyslexic. Others estimate that one in ten of the population has some form of dyslexia. Difficulties range from severe problems with literacy to less obvious difficulties, such as short-term memory loss, sequencing and organising information.

⇨ Dyspraxia: Developmental dyspraxia is an impairment or immaturity of the organisation of movement. This affects the way in which the brain processes information, resulting in messages not being properly or fully transmitted.

⇨ HIV/AIDS: People with HIV/AIDS have impaired immune systems so their bodies have trouble fighting off infections.

Things to consider

The social model of disability rests on the way that society treats disabled people; in other words, people with impairments are disabled through the prejudiced attitudes of society. But what happens if a student can 'pass' for a non-disabled person? Are the problems faced in any way diminished or are there a whole new set of difficult issues to discover?

Not being perceived as disabled might be seen as an advantage by some students as they would avoid being labelled, but on the other hand, a lack of awareness by, for instance, classmates or institution staff, would only add to the difficulties that the student faces. They might not want to consider themselves disabled or disclose their impairment, and therefore will not be able to access the funding and resources they are entitled to.

One of the major problems faced by students who have hidden disabilities is that often other people don't believe them. They are told that they don't look like they are disabled. Many students may feel that the foremost discrimination they face is disbelief. Hidden disabilities can also cause difficulties because of the attitudes of others due to fear or ignorance. People fear what they do not know or understand, or what they cannot see. It is through active campaigning and raising awareness that we can create a society where students with hidden disabilities feel that they can disclose without fear of prejudice or discrimination.

What is the Disability Discrimination Act (DDA)?

⇨ The Disability Discrimination Act creates rights for disabled people.

⇨ Its main focus is on defining who is disabled (part one of the act), employment (part two of the act), access to goods and services (part three of the act) and education (part four of the act).

⇨ Students' Unions cannot afford to be complacent and wait for education institutions to act first to eliminate disability discrimination, or for individual students with disabilities to make complaints about discrimination in education provision.

⇨ A person is protected under the DDA if they come

NATIONAL UNION OF STUDENTS

under the terms of disabled according to the DDA. The DDA says you are a disabled person if you have 'a physical or mental impairment which has a substantial and long-term adverse effect on your ability to carry out normal day-to-day activities'. This can include people with sensory impairments, learning disabilities, cancer, HIV, progressive conditions at the early stage, mental health impairments and conditions which are characterised by a number of cumulative effects such as pain or fatigue.

⇨ You do not have to register as a disabled person to be protected by the legislation.

⇨ The DDA describes discrimination as 'Treating a disabled person less favourably than you would treat someone without a disability, for a reason relating to his or her disability' or failing to make a 'reasonable adjustment'.

More than three million people have asthma in the UK

Looking at the support that your institution provides and questions to be asking

⇨ Is there a recognised and accessible support structure for students with hidden disabilities?

⇨ Are there policies in place with regard to hidden disabilities?

⇨ What is the institution doing about the DDA and how are they including students with hidden disabilities?

⇨ Do an audit of the institution services (look at accessibility, marketing, etc.).

⇨ How well-advertised is funding support like the Disabled Student Allowance for students with hidden disabilities?

⇨ Is there accessible information in conjunction with a source of support and advice?

⇨ How proactive is the institution about hidden disabilities and campaigning and raising awareness?

⇨ See if there is funding for hidden disability projects.

⇨ Do committees within the institution have hidden disabilities as a regular agenda item?

⇨ Are hidden disabilities included in staff and student induction programmes?

⇨ How well publicised is it that students with hidden disabilities have their rights protected under the DDA?

⇨ Does the institution gather the opinions of students with disabilities?

Ways to campaign about hidden disabilities

⇨ Work in partnership with disability co-ordinator, head of student services, etc.

⇨ Campaign to have disability policy in your institution and Students' Union.

⇨ Do hidden disability training that includes students undergoing the training.

⇨ Get a Students with Disabilities Officer/committee/group within your Students' Union.

⇨ Ensure that your Unions' information is available in formats other than standard print.

⇨ Get students to run awareness campaigns – gives them a sense of ownership.

⇨ Work with local organisations and charities on the different awareness days or groups.

⇨ Establish peer mentor and support groups.

⇨ Have student representation on disability groups within your institution.

One in 200 people in the UK has epilepsy. It is a neurological condition characterised by seizures that happen when the electrical system of the brain malfunctions

⇨ Gather the opinions of students with disabilities to see what their thoughts are and if anything needs changing or campaigning for.

⇨ Get email networks going.

⇨ Hold hidden disability training for all those involved in the Students' Union, including executive committee members, staff, bar staff, volunteers, club and society presidents and sport captains.

⇨ Hold quizzes.

⇨ Do a 'Who has the disability?' awareness campaign with posters, flyers, etc.

⇨ Get student champions or campaigners to speak out in lectures etc. or make a film about hidden disabilities to be shown in your institution.

Charities and organisations

⇨ Disability Rights Commission: www.drc-gb.org

⇨ Skill: National Bureau for Disabled Students: www.skill.org.uk

NATIONAL UNION OF STUDENTS

Debenhams first with disabled High Street model

Debenhams breaks the taboo of using disabled model in photography campaign.

By Hilary Alexander

Debenhams has become the first British high-street retailer to break the taboo of using disabled models in campaign photography.

Shannon Murray, 32, who has been confined to a wheelchair since breaking her neck as a teenager, will appear in the store's display window photography and online.

The move follows an approach to Debenhams by Nikki Fox and Natasha Wood, both disability campaigners and presenters of the hit TV show, *How to Look Good Naked With a Difference*.

Shannon will join three other models: Kate Fullman, a size 16 model, Tess Montgomery, a petite 5'4" model, and Tokumbo Daniel, a size 10 model, who will all appear in photographs to promote the recently-launched 'Principles by Ben de Lisi' range which prides itself on its inclusivity. The collection starts at size 8 and goes up to size 20, with a specific petites range as well.

Debenhams is showing an increasing willingness to inject variety into the people modelling its clothes. The new campaign follows hot on the heels of the retail chain using size 16 mannequins in its windows.

Michael Sharp, Debenhams' Deputy Chief Executive, said: 'We cater for women of all shapes and sizes, young and old, non-disabled and disabled, so we wanted our windows to reflect this choice.

'When Nikki and Natasha approached us with the idea, we didn't have to think twice. We are proud to be the first high-street retailer to deliver this. We only wished we had done it sooner', he said.

Nikki Fox praised the store for using Shannon in its campaign: 'I am so happy and proud that Debenhams has used our disabled model for such a massive campaign. It's a really big deal. If seeing Shannon helps another disabled person, then we've done well.'

'Every woman deserves to look good and feel special – which is why there are styles to suit, fit and flatter every body shape in the new Principles range. I think that Shannon looks amazing,' added the designer, Ben de Lisi.

Shannon Murray complimented the retailer for supporting disabled models: 'I think this is a fabulous step forward and I'm proud to be part of such a big move towards positive representation of disability in high-street fashion.'

Debenhams says that it is committed to using disabled models in other photography; a second photographic shoot is being organised.

The images will be used in Debenhams stores in Glasgow, Guildford, Oxford Street in London, and Nottingham, with the intention of rolling out across all stores in the chain.

At London Fashion Week, in September 1998, the late Alexander McQueen made catwalk history by using a model with two specially-carved wooden, prosthetic legs, which he had designed.

The Irish-American model, Aimee Mullins, 23, was the star of the show, in a cream, ruffled-lace skirt and leather bodice. Mullins, a graduate of Georgetown University, and a record-breaking sprinter in disabled games, was born without fibula bones in her shins. Her legs were amputated below the knee when she was one year old. Mullins had previously appeared in an edition of *Dazed & Confused* magazine, which was guest-edited by McQueen.

26 February 2010

© Telegraph Media Group Limited 2010

NATIONAL UNION OF STUDENTS / THE TELEGRAPH

Planes, trains and wheelchairs

Disability doesn't have to mean being stuck at home. Here's our guide to accessible transport – and, remember, if you don't get what you think you're entitled to, don't be afraid to make a complaint.

By Tom Green

Wheelchairs

If your walking difficulties are permanent or near permanent you can get an NHS wheelchair on a free loan – ask your local doctor (GP) for details. The NHS can loan more than one wheelchair if necessary (for example, one for using at home and the other for use at work). It might also be possible to get vouchers from the NHS or, if you get certain benefits, a loan, to help pay for a more expensive wheelchair.

Driving

There are medical standards set for all drivers – you must answer questions on the form when you apply for a provisional licence and you may have to undergo a medical examination. You might need to think about whether you need an adapted car and lessons from a specially trained instructor. When it comes to the test, if you let the Driving Standards Agency know of any special requirements you have it will try to accommodate them.

If you are receiving certain disability benefits it might be possible to get a licence at 16 – ask your benefits advisor for more information.

> *In England, disabled people are entitled to free bus travel at off-peak times on buses. In Wales and Scotland, disabled people and essential companions for disabled people are entitled to a free bus pass*

Motability can sell or hire new or second-hand cars to anyone receiving the higher rate mobility component of disability living allowance. You might also be able to get a free tax disc and, if you're entitled to a Blue Badge, you'll get parking concessions across the UK.

Trains

Although rail operators are legally obliged to make provision for disabled passengers, it's still a good idea to give them at least 24-hours notice if you need assistance. If it's a long journey, start by contacting the train company or, if you have to change services, the main terminal station. The Passenger Transport Executive Group is a good source of local information and advice.

If you have a disability that makes rail travel difficult you might be entitled to a Disabled Persons Railcard, which will give you and a fellow-traveller one-third off most fares (although you'll get the same discounts if you get a 16-25 Railcard).

Buses

In England, disabled people are entitled to free bus travel at off-peak times on buses. In Wales and Scotland, disabled people and essential companions for disabled people are entitled to a free bus pass.

The accessibility of bus services vary, so, if you need assistance, it's best to contact your local Passenger Transport Authority for information. In some areas there are Dial-a-Bus schemes providing door-to-door services for disabled people.

Coaches

Many coaches have high steps that make them inaccessible for some people. However, more accessible vehicles are coming into service and the entire National Express network will be accessible by 2012.

Most companies will not take electric wheelchairs or scooters but they should be willing to take a folding wheelchair if given sufficient notice (they like at least seven days). Some also offer concessionary fares.

In London all newly-licensed taxis must be able to carry a wheelchair and all taxis must be wheelchair-accessible by 1 January 2012

For more information on National Express services you can call its Disabled Persons Travel Helpline on 08717 818179 or textphone on 0121 455 0086.

London Underground

Access for disabled people varies across the Underground, with newer lines and stations tending to have better services. Various sources of help and information are available and you can call the 24-hour travel information centre on 020 7222 1234 or Minicom 020 7918 3015 for help planning your journey.

Taxis and minicabs

Drivers of licensed taxis and minicabs are required to carry a guide dog and hearing dog, or an assistance dog accompanying a person with epilepsy or a physical disability, free of charge. Otherwise there are no legal requirements on accessibility, so speak to your local taxi firms to find one that can meet your needs.

In London all newly-licensed taxis must be able to carry a wheelchair and all taxis must be wheelchair-accessible by 1 January 2012.

Planes

Airlines and travel companies are not allowed by law to refuse to accept bookings from disabled passengers (even if the disability is temporary, such as from an injury). This applies to all flights leaving an airport in the European Union (EU) and to any flight arriving in an EU country on an EU airline.

Airlines have various services for disabled passengers, but if you have a disability and want to fly, it's advisable to contact the travel operator or airline at least 48 hours in advance.

Or, if you're really adventurous, you could even learn to fly yourself.

⇨ The above information is reprinted with kind permission from TheSite.org

© TheSite.org

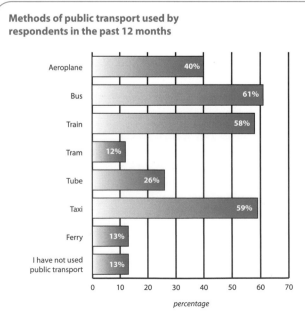

Methods of public transport used by respondents in the past 12 months

- Aeroplane: 40%
- Bus: 61%
- Train: 58%
- Tram: 12%
- Tube: 26%
- Taxi: 59%
- Ferry: 13%
- I have not used public transport: 13%

percentage

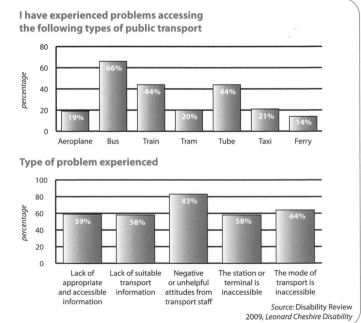

I have experienced problems accessing the following types of public transport

- Aeroplane: 19%
- Bus: 66%
- Train: 44%
- Tram: 20%
- Tube: 44%
- Taxi: 21%
- Ferry: 14%

percentage

Type of problem experienced

- Lack of appropriate and accessible information: 59%
- Lack of suitable transport information: 58%
- Negative or unhelpful attitudes from transport staff: 83%
- The station or terminal is inaccessible: 58%
- The mode of transport is inaccessible: 64%

percentage

Source: Disability Review 2009, Leonard Cheshire Disability

Giving me control of my care has been a revelation

I'm one of the first recipients of the system that lets me spend money on the care of my choice. All that glitters is not gold, but it's been transformative.

By Edward Lawrence*

The Government has a new initiative for disabled people on benefits. It inherited it from the last few months of the Labour Government, but it also ticks a box dear to the heart of the Conservatives: the one that calls for 'more patient power' and more self-reliance. It's 'personalisation'. In a nutshell, it removes the local authority and, in most cases, gives the money straight to the service user to spend as they see fit.

> **In a nutshell, [personalisation] removes the local authority and, in most cases, gives the money straight to the service user to spend as they see fit**

I am one of the first recipients of personalisation and as such I'm seen as a test case. It lets me spend the money I receive on a specialist rehab care provider of my choice, a care provider that sees risk as part of the process of rehabilitation, with support workers who help me set quantifiable goals for improvements.

Not many people argue with personalisation. Isn't it much better to cut out an unnecessary tier of bureaucracy that tells service users what services they need, who provides them and for how long? Who would disagree with greater autonomy for the individual?

As a service user, I have to tell you that all that glitters is not gold. For one thing, the service user has to sort out and provide receipts to agencies accounting where taxpayers' money has gone. But what will happen to these agencies in an era of cuts? Many of them charge a fee to the disabled client, adding insult to injury.

Luckily, I share a home with a friend who knows the system and has not so much gone the extra mile on my behalf as run a marathon in record time. But when they asked the disability agency what assistance they could provide, it explained that the responsibility had been foisted on it at such short notice that it was learning on the job.

We dialled another agency and were informed that a referral from a social worker was required. That would be the same social worker who had given me its number in the first place! Proof that the spirit of Kafka is alive and well and that the Government is sparing no expense keeping it in rude health.

Every social worker is aware of how much political capital has been invested in personalisation by the Government, and it cannot be seen to fail. So social workers cherrypick service users who they think will be the best candidates. Yes, prejudice and social bias even extends to disability.

When I asked my social worker what the drawbacks of personalisation were, he was candid. He admitted it was a process of self-selection. Only those who were erudite, well educated and well organised were encouraged to apply for personalisation and those who led chaotic lives – a euphemism meaning that anyone with drink, drug or mental health issues – was not put forward.

> **Not many people argue with personalisation. Isn't it much better to cut out an unnecessary tier of bureaucracy that tells service users what services they need, who provides them and for how long?**

But if you haven't been put forward for personalisation insist to everyone that you are. It is a good thing. It is suitable for anyone who is organised, methodical and lucid, but it helps immeasurably if someone else is able to assist on your behalf and make sure you are not making any accounting mistakes. Most important, it is suitable for people who are dissatisfied with their current services. It may take a while to bed down but, ultimately, it is worth it. I don't have enough words to describe how much better the new care agency is compared with the old. It will transform your life.

It's your right. Fight, if you have to, to get it.

* Edward Lawrence is a pseudonym.
21 July 2010

© Guardian News and Media Limited 2010

THE GUARDIAN

Disability shouldn't leave children disenfranchised

Finding a suitable school for a child with learning problems can be fraught with difficulty, finds Charlotte Phillips.

'Sometimes I hear other parents fretting about schools and I'd just like to hit them with a shovel,' Louise McDougall says. 'They'll be worrying about whether their child will be stretched academically or if there are enough extra-curricular activities. They don't know they're born. My idea of extra-curricular activity is sitting on the sofa thinking: "Thank God that day is over."'

Louise's son, Mike, is autistic. One of the classic signs is an apparent lack of empathy: the clincher, Louise says, was when she fell down the staircase and four-year-old Mike sat at the top, convulsed with laughter.

> **One state school catering for children with autism has a catchment area that spans an entire county and hundreds of applications each year for a total of just eight or nine places**

Educationally speaking he's one of the lucky ones, diagnosed early and now, aged 15, at a specialist unit in a mainstream local comprehensive. But everything is on a knife edge. Bullying is rife and the attitude of some teachers unhelpful. If Mike can't cope, what happens next?

'I've absolutely no idea,' Louise says. 'You just pray.'

This is the topsy-turvy world of schools for special needs children. For many parents it can feel like a parallel universe where the educational certainties others take for granted are suddenly removed.

If your child has complex learning issues, there may be only a handful of schools that can cater for them. As these schools rarely advertise, let alone go in for all-singing, all-dancing 'look at me' open days, just finding out where they are can require a lot of detective and networking skills.

'Even if you hate socialising, force yourself to network. It's the only way of finding out what's really out there,' says Anna Williams, who estimates she drove 3,000 miles in total in her efforts to track down the ideal school for her son, who has complex hearing and language difficulties. 'Special needs parents tend to know about other schools, even if they're not right for their own child.'

Once you've identified the school, you need to plan a visit. Here, too, the rules are different. 'It's like an 11-plus exam in reverse,' Anna says.

You won't get head teachers vying for your business. You need the right paperwork just to get through the front door. And that doesn't mean glowing reports or top-grade exam results. Instead, parents can be required to paint as black a picture of their child's abilities as possible, backed by reports from experts such as educational psychologists, in order to prove how desperately the place is needed.

But even when you've found the right school, the odds of your child ever taking up a place there can seem overwhelmingly stacked against you.

Special state schools with a good reputation for a particular type of disability are so oversubscribed they make selective grammar schools, with a mere ten or so applicants per place, look like a shoo-in.

THE TELEGRAPH

One state school catering for children with autism has a catchment area that spans an entire county and hundreds of applications each year for a total of just eight or nine places.

And if you decide to try your luck with the private sector, there are also the costs to contend with. Top public schools may have hit the headlines recently with news that they are likely to breach the £30,000 a year barrier, but that's nothing. With fees at some residential schools for severely challenged children reaching £250,000 a year, the million-pound education has already arrived.

In an ideal world, children's educational needs would be cost-blind. Unfortunately for parents, local authorities are caught in an impossible situation. On the one hand they have a legal duty to ensure that children with special needs are given the education that will help them realise their full potential. On the other, they're also required to cough up the funds to pay for it.

Given how tight money is, the result is that instead of parents, schools and local authorities working harmoniously together to find the best possible educational solution for a child, you often get an emotionally draining and drawn-out fight, council officials on one side, purse strings clasped shut, beleaguered parents on the other.

> *Local authorities are caught in an impossible situation. On the one hand they have a legal duty to ensure that children with special needs are given the education that will help them realise their full potential. On the other, they're also required to cough up the funds to pay for it*

It doesn't have to be like this, though, say campaigners for inclusive education. They are convinced that the future for children with special needs lies in bringing them all into mainstream schools.

Head teacher Nigel Utton, who also chairs Heading for Inclusion, has been an advocate of inclusive education since the age of seven when, with other pupils, he spent time at a local special school after his own had flooded.

'We were having playtime and assemblies with them whereas before we'd used the name of that school as a term of abuse. By the time I was a teacher it was firmly set in my brain that to have a decent society we need to learn to live together,' he says.

His school, Bromstone Primary in Kent, is a vision of inclusive education loveliness, where children across the spectrum of educational needs and abilities work together with teachers, sharing an ethos that celebrates every pupil's contribution to the school community.

'With our blind child, the other children will lead him into lunch, make sure he has finished, help him put his tray away, then lead him outside and make sure he has somebody to play with. That hardly requires any money – and it's good for their moral fibre, too,' Utton says.

One of the ways he measures the school's success is down to what he terms the birthday party factor. 'To a child, being invited to birthday parties is a major event. Our children with special needs get invited and invite other people to theirs. And it's not about special needs. They're just friends.'

> ## *In an ideal world, children's educational needs would be cost-blind*

That's something Jo Cameron knows all about. Her son, Tom, who has Down's syndrome, works at a local arts centre and performs with a youth theatre group. Jo, one of the founders of Parents for Inclusion, is convinced that his self-belief is down to a sense of belonging. He went to the same local schools as her other children and has close friends he's known since he was three. 'Tom had the opportunity to be part of his community,' his mother says. 'He still has friends who invite him to parties and their weddings because he went to that local primary.'

Other parents, though, have yet to be convinced. Anna Williams battled her local authority to get funding for a place at an independent residential school when it became clear her son wasn't coping at his state primary. The final straw, she says, was when they pushed him to do SATs.

'He was so traumatised that it took a year before he could see a reading book before bursting into tears,' Anna says.

Today he's in a small class with lessons that are tailored to his needs and is learning. More to the point, he's also happy.

'Mainstream school destroyed his confidence,' Anna says. 'Here he's in a non-scary environment and he's starting to try new things. Last week, he even described his first cricket match to me. For a child like mine, there may be no such thing as a perfect school. But I think we've ended up with the best possible fit.'

* Some names and other details have been changed
21 May 2010

© Telegraph Media Group Limited 2010

Renting with a disability

Jamie Robertson, 25, has cerebral palsy. He explains to TheSite how it can be difficult to find suitable housing if you're a disabled person.

Like many students, when I finished university, I moved back in with my parents in Oxford. I have cerebral palsy, a condition that affects my movement, so I need support with some day-to-day tasks and also use a wheelchair.

I'd been living in accessible accommodation at university, but my parent's house wasn't adapted so there was no accessible toilet or bathroom. I was itching to get my independence back, so when I was offered a job in London, I jumped at it. Unfortunately, things weren't as easy as they looked.

Then, the local authority from the area I wanted to move to in London told me they couldn't give me a care assessment – a process where they assess what support you need and what they're willing to pay for – until I'd lived there for six months. I wanted to move house and I had to delay my start date in the new job while I tried to sort things out. I was so worried that my new employer would think I wasn't interested in the job any more. In total, the two local authorities spent nine months deciding who was going to pay for what. During that time, I was paying for the full cost of my care – £800 a month. I'm still paying this off on my credit card four years later.

Many disabled people have a care package, paid for by their local authority

Many disabled people have a care package, paid for by their local authority, which covers the costs associated with their disability. The job in London meant a move to the capital, but, because I was moving out of their borough, the local authority in Oxford didn't want to continue paying for my care. It was very much a case of 'you're not our responsibility any more'.

It's stressful for anyone to have to move house and there are so many added factors to take into consideration when you're disabled

It's stressful for anyone to have to move house and there are so many added factors to take into consideration when you're disabled. Many landlords aren't aware that there are grants you can apply for to make properties accessible for disabled tenants. My landlady didn't know

Percentage of respondents who own their own home

Yes – 60%   No – 40%

Respondents were asked about their experiences of accessible accommodation:
2% stated that their landlord had refused to allow them to install adaptations.
14% said that barriers related to their impairment mean that they are limited in their choice of accommodation.
14% of respondents said that they could not afford to install necessary adaptations because they could not obtain financial support.
22% stated that there is not enough accessible accommodation in the UK.
15% said that they had experienced difficulties from living in inappropriate accommodation.
41% said that they had made adaptations to their home to make it more suitable.
20% said that they need to make adaptations to their home to make it more suitable for them.

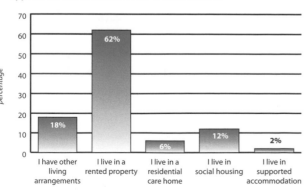

Type of accommodation of non-home owners

- I have other living arrangements: 18%
- I live in a rented property: 62%
- I live in a residential care home: 6%
- I live in social housing: 12%
- I live in supported accommodation: 2%

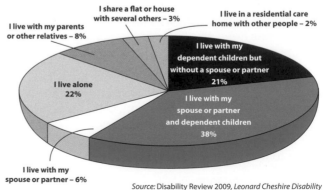

Living circumstances

- I share a flat or house with several others – 3%
- I live in a residential care home with other people – 2%
- I live with my parents or other relatives – 8%
- I live with my dependent children but without a spouse or partner 21%
- I live alone 22%
- I live with my spouse or partner and dependent children 38%
- I live with my spouse or partner – 6%

Source: Disability Review 2009, Leonard Cheshire Disability

THESITE.ORG

this and wasn't happy about many of the changes I needed to make, thinking that they would devalue the property. It's useful to know the grants also cover the costs to put the property back to how it was before when the tenant moves out.

When people are planning buildings, accessibility seems to be regarded as an afterthought

I wanted a wheel-in shower, but we ended up coming to a compromise and she allowed me to put some bars in the bathroom. This means that I'm more dependent on someone else to support me and having a bath rather than a shower means I need someone to help me in and out. I don't really have any privacy because there needs to be someone around and I sometimes feel like I'm living in a goldfish bowl.

When people are planning buildings, accessibility seems to be regarded as an afterthought. The entrance to my flat has been designed around a step entrance and courtyard and there is a lift inside. However, in order to get up to the entrance, there is an outdoor lift. It's prone to all the elements and often breaks down as a result. Not only was it expensive to install but it's also expensive to repair. I'm sure if they'd asked a disabled person, they would have told them a ramp is much more convenient and obviously a lot cheaper.

When I wanted to move again, one estate agent came back to me with a property on Caledonian Road saying 'It's wheelchair-accessible – there's only four steps outside, so as long as you can walk, it's wheelchair-accessible.' It just shows many people don't understand disability or the needs of disabled people.

And once again I had problems with the care package, even though I was only moving down the road. The new flat was in a different borough, so I had to have another assessment – and another eight months passed before I saw any results. It makes you feel guilty for needing support and that's not the sort of situation anyone should be put in.

There are ways to improve things. As disabled people we need to make sure our voices are heard and we have a say in the way we live our lives. I now work as a Local Campaigns Officer at the disability charity Scope. I support individual disabled people who are campaigning for change on an issue in their local community, whether it's access to a restaurant or on public transport.

There are ways to improve things. As disabled people we need to make sure our voices are heard and we have a say in the way we live our lives

I'd also like to see more disabled people on property planning boards and more disabled people being listened to by their councillors. Involving us in the process would mean the decisions made would genuinely work for us. There could also be improvements made to the way care packages are assessed. A single assessment that all local authorities could use would cut costs and make it easier to move house.

As told to Louis Pattison

⇨ The above information is reprinted with kind permission from TheSite.org

© TheSite.org

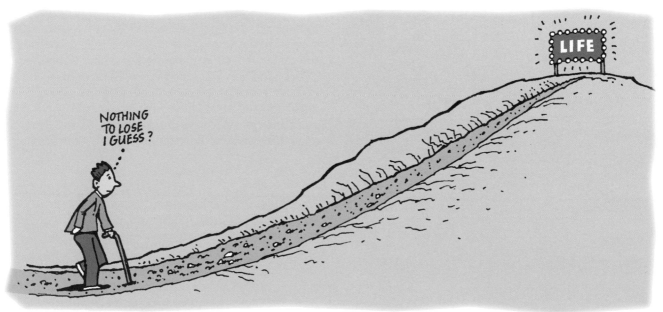

NOTHING TO LOSE I GUESS?

LIFE

Siblings of disabled young people

Information from Sibs.

The needs of young siblings

Most young siblings experience lack of parental attention, isolation, ignorance about disability, difficulty coping with their experiences, and the financial impact of disability on the family. Many studies on siblings of children with a chronic illness indicate that siblings are at risk of negative psychological effects. When we talk to siblings, parents and professionals, the picture that emerges is that many siblings are struggling to cope with the emotional and practical demands that being a sibling entails. Even though they have these needs that require attention at different stages of their lives, young siblings are often marginalised by their families, society and service providers.

Lack of parental attention

Siblings grow up in a family where, regardless of the age of the sibling, the majority of family resources, parental attention, and professional services are directed, indefinitely, towards another child (i.e. the disabled child). Throughout their lives, siblings' needs come second to those of another person. Many siblings feel that they get a lot less attention from their

parents compared to their disabled brother or sister. In the majority of families the attention gap is real, yet even when parents do all they can to share attention out, siblings still feel that they get less attention. As a result, siblings often experience feelings such as intense jealousy, resentment towards their disabled brother or sister, and believe that they are not seen to be as important or special as their brother or sister. Siblings may receive more negative attention from parents than peers in a similar situation. Parental depression and anxiety is prevalent in parents of disabled children and affects the amount and quality of attention parents can provide. Other parents devote huge amounts of time to disability causes which can take their time away from siblings. Significant loss of parental attention will have negative implications for siblings' self-esteem, academic performance, and behavioural and emotional development. Siblings themselves can have their own health and learning needs overlooked, as they may not appear significant in comparison to those of the disabled child.

Ignorance about the disability or condition

Siblings rarely receive accurate and age-appropriate information about their brother or sister's disability or medical condition. It is common for siblings to lack the basic knowledge and information they need to understand the circumstances in which they find themselves; in the absence of accurate and appropriate information they may develop their own theories to make sense of their situation. This can be the cause of self-blame and guilt and a range of erroneous views that can extend even into adulthood. In situations where disabled children with challenging behaviour hurt siblings or damage their belongings, siblings often believe that this is because the disabled child doesn't like them; this 'taking it personally' will continue until the sibling has a full understanding of the condition and its effect on behaviour. Siblings of children with life-limiting conditions are least likely to be well informed about their brother or sister's condition, even though children who are informed about prognosis show less anxiety than those who are not informed.

Isolation

Until siblings meet other siblings at sibling groups they often believe that they are the only ones. It is not enough to point out another sibling and say that 'He or she also has a brother with autism.' Siblings need to hear other children talking about their experiences of family life in order to really know that other people understand what it is like for them. The majority of adult siblings who contact

SIBS

Sibs have an average age of 40 – the stage in their lives when they need support with future care issues. Their sense of relief at being able to talk to another adult sibling is palpable; almost always having their unique experiences and feelings validated for the first time. 40 years is too long to feel you have to cope alone; it is not acceptable for parents of disabled children and should not be acceptable for siblings either. Difficulty with having friends back to their home can limit opportunities for time with peer group outside of school.

Statistics about carers in England, Wales, Scotland and Northern Ireland. Numbers of carers, all ages. (Source, Census 2001)

Region	Number of carers	% of total population (all ages)
England	4,877,060	10%
Northern Ireland	185,086	11%
Scotland	481,579	10%
Wales	340,745	11%
UK total	5,884,450	10%

Region	Number of carers providing 50+ hours care per week	% of all carers providing 50+ hours care per week
England	998,732	20%
Northern Ireland	46,912	25%
Scotland	115,674	24%
Wales	89,604	26%
UK total	1,250,922	21%

Source: Facts about carers policy briefing, June 2009, Carers UK (www.carersuk.org)

Difficulty coping

Siblings can experience challenges that other children do not and they regularly find themselves in situations that can be difficult to manage; situations such as dealing with a brother or sister's challenging behaviour or coping with feeling embarrassed in public when people stare. A study of adolescent siblings of children with severe disabilities found all were struggling to cope with their situation. Many young siblings can give the appearance of coping during childhood and indeed seeming more mature and well-adjusted than peers. At sibling groups, however, it often becomes apparent that many coping siblings have internalised their feelings. Siblings, through their close relationship with the disabled child, often experience prejudice, bullying, limited family activities and exclusion from mainstream activities. The extent to which siblings manage to cope can crucially depend on their individual character and resilience. The situation can be exacerbated if the parents/carers themselves have difficulty coping and cannot adequately support the siblings. Many siblings are young carers, providing help with things like personal care, communication, translation at medical appointments, and entertaining their disabled brothers and sisters. About a third of children at young carers' projects in the UK are siblings. Siblings of children with a life-limiting condition have to deal with the additional issues of anticipatory grief and bereavement, and often grow up in 'houses of chronic sorrow'. Over a third of Sibs enquiries are from or about siblings of children with autism, a group of siblings who may be at increased risk of negative impact due to the nature of the disability and its effect on family dynamics and family stress levels.

Financial impact

Siblings are more likely than their peer group to be raised within a family that experiences poverty; 93% of families of disabled children in the UK are struggling financially. Family expenditure to meet the needs of the disabled child means that fewer resources are available for the needs of siblings.

Positive aspects of being a sibling

Being the sibling of a disabled child can also bring positives, such as increased maturity, increased tolerance of others and enhanced communication skills. However, these skills and attributes may be acquired at a cost of the above to siblings.

More research is needed

There is a need for further research on the needs of young siblings who currently have a disabled brother or sister. The variables that affect psychological adjustment in siblings are wide ranging – such as the parents' ability to cope, the sibling's temperament, the nature of the disability, the family's communication style, parental depression, amount of caregiving required for the disabled child, and the amount of care being provided by siblings. From our experience it would seem that being a sibling today is harder now than it was 20 or even ten years ago due to the increased numbers of disabled children with complex medical needs, the diminished availability of extended family for support, the inadequacy of services for families of disabled children, and the fact that the majority of siblings are the only sibling in the family.

⇨ The above information is reprinted with kind permission from Sibs. Visit www.sibs.org.uk for more.

© Sibs

SIBS

Disability discrimination

This information applies to England, Wales, Scotland and Northern Ireland.

Discrimination because of disability

It is against the law to discriminate against disabled people in various areas of their lives.

For example, it is against the law to discriminate against disabled people at work (see under heading Disability discrimination at work), and when providing goods, facilities and services (see under heading Access to goods, facilities and services). There is also limited protection against discrimination for disabled people who are renting or buying property (see under heading Discrimination when buying or renting property), and in education (see under heading Discrimination in education).

There are some important areas where it is not against the law to discriminate against disabled people, for example access to public transport services.

Disability discrimination at work

It is against the law for an employer:

⇨ to discriminate directly against you if you are disabled or because you are associated with someone who is disabled; for example, your partner or child.

⇨ to treat you less favourably because of your disability – including recruitment and selection, terms and conditions, dismissal and redundancy (but see below).

⇨ not to make reasonable adjustments to the workplace to enable you to work or to continue to work (see below).

⇨ to harass you if you are disabled; for example, by making jokes about your disability.

⇨ to victimise you if you take legal action because of discrimination against you, or if you help someone else to take legal action because of discrimination.

Employers can treat disabled people less favourably only if they have a sufficiently justifiable reason for doing so, and only if the problem cannot be overcome by making 'reasonable adjustments'. For example, an employer would be justified in rejecting someone with severe back pain for a job as a carpet fitter, as they cannot carry out the essential requirements of the job.

Examples of the types of adjustments that an employer might make include:

⇨ making physical adjustments to the premises.

⇨ supplying special equipment to help you do your job.

⇨ transferring you to a different post or work place.

⇨ altering your hours of work or giving you extra time off.

When employers are deciding whether an adjustment is reasonable they can take into account several things, including the cost of making an adjustment and the size of their business. If you are already in the job, your employer can also take into account your skills and experience and the length of time you have worked there.

Access to Work

If you are disabled and need changes at work so you can do your job you may be able to get help from Access to Work. You may also be able to get help from Access to Work if you are disabled and are looking for a job. Access to Work is a Government scheme that works with disabled people and employers to work out what changes are needed so the disabled person can do their job. They may also be able to provide some money to pay for the changes. Access to Work may be able to provide an assessment of your needs at work, and help with things like equipment, adapting premises or a support worker. As the employee or person looking for work, it is your responsibility to contact Access to Work.

For more information about Access to Work, ask at your local Jobcentre Plus, or look on the Directgov website at: www.direct.gov.uk

In Northern Ireland, for more information about Access to Work, ask at your local Jobs and Benefits office or JobCentre, or look on the NIDirect website at: www.nidirect.gov.uk

If you have suffered discrimination at work because of your disability, you should talk to an experienced adviser; for example, at a Citizens Advice Bureau.

Other types of discrimination

As well as being treated unfairly because of a disability, you could be treated unfairly for other reasons because:

⇨ you're a woman.

⇨ of your race, ethnic origin or nationality.

⇨ you're lesbian or gay.

⇨ of your age.

⇨ of your religion.

For example, you're a disabled woman who's been sacked because you're pregnant. You may have a claim for sex discrimination as well as disability discrimination. If you think you've been treated unfairly because you're disabled and because you're a woman, make sure you raise both issues if you make a complaint.

Access to goods, facilities and services

The law gives certain basic rights to all consumers of goods, facilities and services.

In addition to your basic rights as a consumer, if you are disabled, you also have other rights which protect you against discrimination when you buy goods and services or use certain facilities. This applies regardless of the size of the organisation or company providing the goods, services or facilities.

Examples of services which must not discriminate against you if you are disabled include services provided by: hotels, banks, building societies, solicitors, local authorities, advice agencies, pubs, theatres, shops, telesales, railway stations, churches, doctors, law courts and public transport. It does not matter whether the service is free or has to be paid for.

Generally speaking, insurance companies are not allowed to discriminate against you if you are disabled, but they may sometimes be able to treat you less favourably if they can show that this is based on reliable information about insurance risk.

What you can expect from providers of goods, facilities and services

Providers of goods, facilities and services must not treat you less favourably than they would treat a person who is not disabled (unless they can show that the treatment is justified). An example of less favourable treatment is where a hotel refuses a booking from a person with a hearing impairment, saying that the hotel is not suitable for people with a hearing impairment.

Service providers must make 'reasonable adjustments' to allow a disabled person to use their services. If they don't do this, they must be able to show that their failure to do so is justified. Examples of making reasonable adjustments include providing information on audiotape as well as in writing, or installing a ramp to allow wheelchair access.

The Government has produced a Code of Practice about disability discrimination. It is a statement of good practice which you can use when dealing with someone who provides goods, facilities or services. If you decide to take legal action because you have suffered disability discrimination, the court must consider the Code when it arrives at a decision. A copy of the Code is available from the website of the Equality and Human Rights Commission at: www.equalityhumanrights.com

The Equality and Human Rights Commission has a guide to taking court action for disability discrimination which you can get from their website.

If you think a provider of goods, facilities or services has discriminated against you because you are disabled, you should talk to an experienced adviser; for example, at a Citizens Advice Bureau.

Discrimination when buying or renting property

The law gives certain basic rights to everyone who buys or rents property.

In England, Wales and Scotland, for more information about your basic rights when you rent a property, if it

is a private sector landlord see Renting from a private landlord on the Adviceguide website.

In England and Wales, if it is a social housing landlord, see Renting from a social housing landlord. In Scotland if it is a public sector landlord, see Renting from a public sector landlord on the Adviceguide website.

In addition to your basic rights, if you are disabled, you also have other rights which protect you against discrimination when you buy or rent property. Someone who rents or sells you property may be discriminating against you if:

⇨ they refuse to sell or rent a property to you.

⇨ they offer you a property for sale or rent on worse terms than they would to a person who is not disabled.

⇨ they treat you less favourably on a housing waiting list than a person who is not disabled.

⇨ you are renting and they unreasonably prevent you from using benefits or facilities or don't allow you to use these facilities in the same way as other tenants do.

⇨ you are renting and they evict or harass you for a reason connected with your disability.

Landlords who rent out accommodation in their own homes are allowed to discriminate against people with disabilities.

Services such as estate agents must make their offices accessible, as long as it is reasonable to do so.

A landlord's duty to make alterations for disabled people

If you're disabled, you can ask your landlord (or future landlord) to make certain changes to the property, and to their policies, when this is necessary for you to be able to live in the property. These changes are known as reasonable adjustments. Landlords who refuse to make reasonable adjustments, and who cannot justify this, are discriminating against you and they are breaking the law.

Reasonable adjustments can include:

⇨ providing aids and services, such as a copy of the tenancy agreement in Braille or a temporary ramp for a wheelchair user with a small step up to their flat;

⇨ changing practices, policies or procedures. An example of this would be to change the parking policy so that a disabled occupier who has difficulty walking can park in front of the building;

⇨ changing a term in the letting agreement. An example of this would be changing a term in the letting agreement which says that tenants can't make improvements so that a disabled person could make a disability-related improvement. Another example would be changing a term which bans pets for a disabled person who has an assistance dog.

What is reasonable will depend on the individual circumstances, including:

⇨ the type and length of your letting;

⇨ how much difference the adjustment will make to you;

⇨ how much money your landlord has.

Your landlord doesn't have to take any steps that involve the removal or alteration of physical features; for example, putting in a permanent concrete ramp or major works which would involve serious damage to the property.

Your landlord must not discriminate against you, for example, by evicting you or increasing the rent because of the cost of the adjustment.

If you think you have been discriminated against when buying or renting a property because you are disabled, you should talk to an experienced adviser; for example, at a Citizens Advice Bureau.

Discrimination in education

(This information applies to England, Wales and Scotland only.)

In England, Wales and Scotland, providers of education must not discriminate against disabled students, or disabled people applying to be students. Providers of education include providers of further education, higher education, adult and community education. This does not apply to Northern Ireland.

Providers of education must not discriminate against students or applicants in the following ways:

Less favourable treatment

Providers of education must not discriminate against students or applicants by treating them less favourably than students who are not disabled, unless they can justify this treatment (see below). This means that education providers must not:

⇨ refuse to offer a disabled student a place because they are disabled, or offer them a place on less favourable terms than a student who is not disabled.

⇨ treat a disabled student less favourably in any aspect of educational life, including trips, excursions and extra-curricular activities.

⇨ exclude a disabled student from school because of their disability.

For example, if a school refuses to take a child who suffers from epilepsy unless she stops having fits, this will count as discrimination.

In some cases, an education provider can treat a disabled student less favourably if it can justify this. A school can justify less favourable treatment if it is because of a permitted form of selection. For example, a child with

learning difficulties applies to a school that selects its intake on the basis of academic ability and fails the school's entrance exam. Under these circumstances, the school would be able to justify not offering the child a place.

Making reasonable adjustments

Providers of education must not discriminate against disabled students or applicants by failing to make reasonable adjustments to allow for their disability. If this places a disabled student at a substantial disadvantage compared with students who are not disabled, this will be regarded as discrimination. For example, a deaf pupil who lip-reads is at a disadvantage if teachers continue to speak while facing away to write on a whiteboard.

Making reasonable adjustments includes providing special aids such as equipment and sign language interpreters.

There are some circumstances in which an education provider may be able to justify not making an adjustment for a student's disability.

Schools do not have to make reasonable adjustments to buildings and the physical environment of the school. However, all local education authorities in England, Wales and Scotland must have plans to make their schools more accessible to disabled pupils. Maintained schools, independent schools and non-maintained special schools must produce their own accessibility plans. The plans must be in writing and publicly available.

Providers of further and higher education do have to make reasonable adjustments to their premises to allow better access for disabled students. However, issues such as cost can be taken into account when they decide whether an adjustment is reasonable.

For more information about the rights of disabled students at school or in post-16 education, visit the website of the Equality and Human Rights Commission at: www.equalityhumanrights.com

Providing for children with special educational needs

All schools must comply with a statement of special educational needs where one has been issued for a child. For example, a school must recruit a learning support assistant or provide information in Braille or audio tape where the student's statement provides for one. In some cases, colleges of further education must also comply with a statement of special educational needs.

What action can you take about discrimination in education?

If you have a child who has special needs, in England, you may be able to complain to the First-tier Tribunal (Special Educational Needs and Disability). The Tribunal publishes a guide to bring a disability discrimination case.

This is available on the Tribunal website at: www.sendist. gov.uk. The Tribunal also has a helpline. The number is: 0870 241 2555.

In Wales, you can complain to the Special Educational Needs Tribunal for Wales. You can find information about discrimination appeals on the Tribunal's website at: www.wales.gov.uk

In Scotland, you can complain to the Appeal Committee of the local education authority.

For more information about the rights of disabled students at school or in post-16 education and what action you can take if you want to make a complaint, visit the website of the Equality and Human Rights Commission at: www.equalityhumanrights.com

If you think you have suffered discrimination in education because of your disability, you should talk to an experienced adviser; for example, at a Citizens Advice Bureau.

Access to public transport

If you're disabled, providers of public transport must not treat you less favourably than they would treat a person who isn't disabled (unless they can show that the treatment is justified). They have the same duties as other providers of services. These rules apply to the transport service itself as well as to other related services; for example, at a railway station.

There are exceptions these rules – ships are not covered by the rules although their related services are. For example, if you're disabled, you must not be treated less favourably at the ferry port.

When you travel by air, airport operators must provide services which allow you to board, disembark and transfer to another flight. They are not allowed to charge for these services.

There are also special rules protecting disabled passengers when they travel by air in Europe. Airlines and travel companies are not allowed to refuse to accept bookings from disabled passengers. This applies to all flights leaving an airport in the European Union (EU) and to any flight arriving in an EU country on an EU airline.

The Government has issued guidelines for transport providers on good practice for serving disabled customers. You can get the guidelines from the Equality and Human Rights Commission (EHRC) website at: www.equalityhumanrights.com

⇨ The above information is reprinted by kind permission of Citizens Advice. Visit their Adviceguide website at www.adviceguide.org.uk for more information.

© Citizens Advice. Citizens Advice is an operating name of the National Association of Citizens Advice Bureaux

Employment rights and the Disability Discrimination Act

Disabled workers share the same general employment rights as other workers, but there are also some special provisions for them under the Disability Discrimination Act (DDA). One important aspect of this is the right to reasonable adjustments in the workplace.

The Disability Discrimination Act

Under the DDA, it is unlawful for employers to discriminate against disabled people for a reason related to their disability, in all aspects of employment, unless this can be justified. The Act covers things like:

⇨ application forms;

⇨ interview arrangements;

⇨ proficiency tests;

⇨ job offers;

⇨ terms of employment;

⇨ promotion, transfer or training opportunities;

⇨ work-related benefits such as access to recreation or refreshment facilities;

⇨ dismissal or redundancy;

⇨ deciding pay;

⇨ training and development;

⇨ discipline and grievances;

⇨ countering bullying and harassment.

Reasonable adjustments in the workplace

Under the DDA, your employer has a duty to make 'reasonable adjustments' to make sure you're not put at a substantial disadvantage by employment arrangements or any physical feature of the workplace.

Examples of the sort of adjustments your employer should consider, in consultation with you, include:

⇨ allocating some of your work to someone else;

⇨ transferring you to another post or another place of work;

⇨ making adjustments to the buildings where you work;

⇨ being flexible about your hours – allowing you to have different core working hours and to be away from the office for assessment, treatment or rehabilitation;

⇨ providing training or retraining if you cannot do your current job any longer;

⇨ providing modified equipment;

⇨ making instructions and manuals more accessible;

⇨ providing a reader or interpreter.

Things to consider at work

You can play an active role in discussing these arrangements with your employer. You might also want to encourage your employer to speak to someone with expertise in providing work-related help for disabled people, such as an occupational health adviser.

Issues for you both to consider include:

⇨ how effective will an adjustment be?

⇨ will it mean that your disability is slightly less of a disadvantage or will it significantly reduce the disadvantage?

⇨ is it practical?

⇨ will it cause much disruption?

⇨ will it help other people in the workplace?

⇨ is it affordable?

You may want to make sure that your employer is aware of the Access to Work programme run by Jobcentre Plus. Through this programme, employers can get advice on appropriate adjustments and possibly some financial help towards the cost of the adjustments.

Redundancy

Your employer cannot select you for redundancy because you are disabled or for any reason relating to your disability. If your employer is consulting about any future redundancies, they should take reasonable steps to make sure you are included in the consultations.

Your employer must also make reasonable adjustments to any selection criteria they create for selecting employees for redundancies, to make sure the criteria do not discriminate against disabled employees. For example, a reasonable adjustment for your employer to make could be discounting disability-related sickness

absence when using attendance as part of their redundancy selection scheme.

The Equality and Human Rights Commission

The Equality and Human Rights Commission is a good source of advice if you feel you may have been discriminated against at work or elsewhere. It can also help if you think you have been discriminated against and want to lodge a claim at an Employment Tribunal.

⇨ The above information is reprinted with kind permission from Directgov. Visit www.direct.gov.uk for more information.

© Crown copyright

Disabled people's access to goods and services

Ipsos MORI survey for Leonard Cheshire Disability.

A recent survey conducted by Ipsos MORI on behalf of Leonard Cheshire Disability looked at disabled people's experience of accessing goods and services, and their awareness of Part 3 of the Disability Discrimination Act (which specifies disabled people's rights regarding access to goods and services).

Key findings

⇨ Two in five (40%) disabled people have experienced difficulties accessing goods and services in the last twelve months, with around a quarter of all disabled people (23%) directly identifying their experiences as discriminatory.

⇨ The difficulties they experienced included:

↳ lack of appropriate facilities (15% mention);

↳ difficulty using public transport (16% mention);

↳ difficulty in entering or getting around premises such as shops, banks and hotels (13% mention).

⇨ Around a quarter (28%) of disabled people who had experienced difficulty in accessing goods and services have taken some sort of action to challenge this. The actions taken included:

↳ talking to a member of staff about the issue (17% mention);

↳ making a formal complaint to the organisation (12% mention);

↳ not using the shop or service again (12% mention);

↳ taking legal action (1% mention only). In contrast, one in eight (12%) disabled people who have not experienced difficulties accessing goods and services in the last 12 months say they would take or consider taking legal action against a service provider in the future if they felt they were treated unfairly/differently to people without a disability.

⇨ Approaching two in five (37%) disabled people do not feel they know enough about the law to challenge unfair treatment in the provision of goods and services. In particular, one in five (20%) disabled people say they have never heard of the Disability Discrimination Act and around half (51%) of disabled people have heard of it, but feel they know 'not very much' or 'nothing at all' about it.

⇨ Almost three in five (57%) disabled people do not think they would be able to afford the cost of taking legal action.

⇨ Three-quarters (76%) of disabled people agree that shops and providers would make their services more accessible if they felt they might face legal action.

Technical note

⇨ A total of 1,095 disabled people were identified and interviewed face-to-face over four waves of Ipsos MORI's weekly Omnibus service (Capibus). Capibus interviews a nationally representative quota sample of adults throughout Great Britain aged 15+. Two screener questions were used to establish disability status (based on the Disability Discrimination Act definition), and hence eligibility for the rest of the questions from a total sample of 7,680 Capibus respondents.

⇨ Interviews were conducted between 13 November and 10 December 2009.

⇨ Those identified as eligible for this survey retained the weights allocated to them as part of the overall Capibus weighting scheme, in which the data for all 7,680 respondents was weighted to reflect the known profile of the adult population in GB for age, social grade, region and work status – within gender, plus tenure and ethnicity.

14 April 2010

⇨ The above information is an extract from Ipsos MORI's report *Disabled People's Access to Goods and Services*, and is reprinted with permission. Visit www.ipsos-mori.com for more information.

© Ipsos MORI

Disability two ticks symbol

What is the Disability Symbol?

It's a recognition given by Jobcentre Plus to employers based in Great Britain who have agreed to take action to meet five commitments regarding the employment, retention, training and career development of disabled employees.

How is the Symbol relevant to me as a jobseeker or employee?

There are employers all over Great Britain who use the Disability Symbol. They range from small to very large organisations in all different types of business. Symbol-using employers make five commitments regarding the employment, retention, training and career development of disabled people.

What commitments do employers make?

Employers who use the Symbol have agreed with Jobcentre Plus that they will take action on these five commitments:

1. to interview all disabled applicants who meet the minimum criteria for a job vacancy and consider them on their abilities.

2. to ensure there is a mechanism in place to discuss,

at any time, but at least once a year, with disabled employees what can be done to make sure they can develop and use their abilities.

3. to make every effort when employees become disabled to make sure they stay in employment.

4. to take action to ensure that all employees develop the appropriate level of disability awareness needed to make these commitments work.

5. to annually review the five commitments and what has been achieved, plan ways to improve on them and let employees and Jobcentre Plus know about progress and future plans.

How will I recognise the Disability Symbol?

The Disability Symbol is a circular symbol, usually green, with two ticks.

What vacancies does the Disability Symbol apply to?

All vacancies based in Great Britain (GB) where the employer has been awarded the Disability Symbol. It is only applicable to vacancies where the posts will be located in England, Scotland or Wales. Employers that use the Symbol, but are advertising vacancies based outside of GB are not obliged to use the Disability Symbol criteria during recruitment.

What does it mean if I see the Disability Symbol on a job advert?

It means the employer will guarantee to interview you if you meet the minimum criteria for that job. Find out from the employer what the minimum criteria are. That way, you'll have a good idea of whether it's worth applying and what to expect.

Where else might I see the Disability Symbol?

You might see it in the vacancy section of a newspaper, or on a vacancy displayed on a Jobpoint, or on application forms or papers sent to you by an employer.

What if I am employed by the Council?

This means you'll have the opportunity to say if you feel

WALTHAM FOREST COUNCIL

that more can be done to develop you to enable you to use your abilities fully. The guaranteed interview promise also applies to internal vacancies advertised within your organisation, provided that you meet the minimum criteria for the job.

What happens if I become disabled or there are changes to my disability whilst working for my employer?

If this should happen and there are aspects of your present employment that make it difficult for you to carry on in the same work, as a symbol user your employer will do all they can to make sure you can stay in a job.

How does the Disability Discrimination Act (DDA) affect disability symbol-using employers?

Symbol-using employers are covered by the DDA in the same way as other employers. The action that they take as a symbol user is in addition to any obligations placed on them by the Act, and in no way affects your rights as a disabled person under this Act.

24 June 2009

⇨ Information from Waltham Forest Council. Visit www.walthamforest.gov.uk for more information.

© *Waltham Forest Council 2010*

Equality Bill passed by Parliament

ECU welcomes bold step forward in tackling discrimination.

ECU welcomes the news that MPs approved the Equality Bill last night (6 April 2010).

There were fears that the Bill might have been watered down as a result of the dissolution of Parliament in the run-up to the general election. However, all major provisions within the Bill have remained intact. Amendments tabled in the House of Lords have been incorporated into the final version of the Bill.

Once it receives Royal Assent, the Bill will become the Equality Act 2010. Very few provisions within the Equality Act will be implemented immediately, as most need to be enacted by ministers after the general election.

The majority of the new legislation is expected to come in to force in autumn this year, with the general public duty (a duty placed on public bodies including higher education institutions to proactively promote equality) more likely to follow from April 2011.

The Equality Act seeks to:

Consolidate and streamline current anti-discrimination legislation

Nine major pieces of primary anti-discrimination legislation and around 100 statutory instruments are being consolidated into one Act.

Introduce a range of new specific measures that will have direct implications for higher education institutions

Including an extended definition of positive action to enable employers to address significant patterns of under-representation amongst their staff, the publication of gender pay gap data by individual HEIs, a ban on the use of pre-employment health questionnaires and extended legal protection for women when breast-feeding.

Make the law more explicit...

...in the extent to which it covers the 'protected characteristics' of pregnancy and maternity, marital or civil partnership and gender reassignment status.

Make it easier for people to bring cases of discrimination and extending the powers of employment tribunals

It will be possible for people to bring cases of 'dual discrimination' (for example, discrimination on the grounds that a person is a black woman or a Muslim man) and enable tribunals to make broader recommendations for employers in response to the circumstances of an individual case of discrimination.

Welcoming the news, Levi Pay, Policy Director at ECU said:

'This legislation goes much further than a statutory tidying-up exercise – it is a bold step forward in tackling discrimination.

'Some of the measures will require concrete actions from HEIs, such as the ban on using pre-employment health questionnaires and the proposed publication of employers' gender pay gaps.

'Under the new anti-discrimination legislation, it will be clear if organisations aren't complying with their legal responsibilities. It has never been more important for HEIs to ensure they are adequately resourcing their work to promote equality.'

7 April 2010

⇨ Information from the Equality Challenge Unit. Visit www.ecu.ac.uk for more information.

© *Equality Challenge Unit*

WALTHAM FOREST COUNCIL / EQUALITY CHALLENGE UNIT

Mind your language

Words can cause terrible damage. When did people with disabilities cease to matter in the battle against bigotry?

By Ian Birrell

Racism was rife in the playgrounds of my youth. It seems incredible looking back, but if someone would not share their sweets or lend a few pennies to a friend in need of crisps, they might be mocked as 'Jews'. Or even 'Yids'. Sometimes, children would go so far as to rub their noses in a 'Shylock' gesture to emphasise the point.

It must have been hellish for the handful of Jewish pupils. Thankfully, as we grew older and began to learn the brutal history of anti-Semitism, the taunts dried up. Today, such behaviour is stamped upon. A lexicon of loathsome words has been driven underground as we make faltering steps forward towards a more tolerant society.

Sticks and stones break bones, but words wound. This explains why there are such howls of outrage when a low-rent celebrity makes a joke about 'Pakis', or when a newspaper columnist delivers a diatribe against homosexuals. Casual racism, crude stereotyping and abuse towards a minority is not just offensive, but corrosive.

So why is it acceptable against people with disabilities? When did they become such a forgotten minority that they ceased to matter in the battle against bigotry? A group so exiled still from mainstream society that it has become acceptable to fling around hateful words such as 'retard' and 'spazz' without a murmur of disquiet. Not just in the playground, where these words and many more like them are commonplace, but online, in the office, in the home and in Hollywood.

This week we had two of the hottest young actors, Robert Pattinson and Kristen Stewart, describe rumours of their romance as 'so retarded'. Last month, Guy Ritchie used the same word to describe his former wife. Previously, it was Lindsay Lohan, Courtney Love, Russell Brand and Britney Spears. Imagine how their careers would have nose-dived if they used language offensive to gay or black people.

Go on to YouTube and look at all the videos of people dancing 'like a retard'. Or go on to MySpace and find an oh-so-funny gallery entitled 'Adopt Your Own Retard'. Or go on to any one of dozens of Internet sites and laugh at the jokes about 'retards'. Or go on to the most popular political blogs and see the word bandied around as a term of abuse; one left-leaning site failed to spot the irony of a rant about 'homophobic, racist retards' in a recent posting on the BNP.

It is not just the new media polluted by such unthinking contempt. Listen to radio phone-in shows. Or watch the film *Tropic Thunder*, which uses 'retard' or 'retarded' 17 times and makes gags about actors going the 'full retard'. Or check out the Black Eyed Peas song 'Let's Get Retarded' with its chorus 'Everybody, Everybody, Let's get into it, Get stupid, Get retarded'. This from a band whose main creative force was one of the most influential figures behind the mobilisation of support for the election of Barack Obama as President of the United States.

But then, even the first black president makes derogatory jokes about the disabled, while a leading French politician yesterday used autism as a form of political abuse against the Tories, and a supposedly-liberal newspaper splashed it across its front page without comment.

In America, the fightback has begun. The Special Olympics has launched a campaign to drive the word 'retard' into disuse, asking people to pledge never to use the word. Many of the pledges are from children such as Samantha, who has a sister with special needs. 'All my life I have heard people saying the r-word. It makes me really upset. No one understands how hurtful it is until you have someone close to you being called that.'

As the parent of a child with profound mental and physical disabilities, I share Samantha's view. It is deeply upsetting to hear words once used to describe my daughter thrown around as a casual insult. But far worse than my own bruised sensitivities, language reflects how we view the world, reinforcing the exclusion of people with disabilities from the rest of society.

When people with physical disabilities are figures of fun and mental incapacity is a term of insult, is it any wonder my daughter gets unpleasant stares wherever she goes? Is it any wonder parents complain over the appearance of a children's television presenter missing part of one arm? Or a major fashion chain insists that a similarly-

disabled worker is hidden out of sight of customers? Or that a college allows classmates to hold a vote to ban a student with Down's syndrome from a barbecue party, as happened this summer?

People should bear in mind that barely one in six disabled people are born with their disability, and the number of people with disabilities is rising. Despite this, there is so little interaction with disabled people that a recent survey by Scope discovered a majority of Britons believe most people see them as inferior people. Given this scarcely-believable finding, it is unsurprising that people with disabilities find it so much harder to get jobs, are far more likely to live in poverty, will be paid less and bullied more if they do find work and, increasingly, are victims of hate crime.

Six weeks ago, Britain was engulfed in outrage over the terrible story of Fiona Pilkington, who killed herself and her disabled daughter after years of hostility from her neighbours. But the reality is that disabled people are regularly mocked, taunted, harassed, hurt and humiliated, with the most vulnerable – those with mental disability – suffering the worst. There are even cases of torture and disembowelment, of a woman urinated on and filmed as she lay dying in a doorway.

Hate crime is the most extreme articulation of the prejudice that disabled people endure on a daily basis. Its roots lie in contempt, fertilised by misguided feelings of superiority. So will anything really change while retard is an acceptable term of abuse, and autism is used to denigrate political rivals?

'We are giving people permission to say and do hateful things,' said John Knight, director of policy and campaigns at Leonard Cheshire Disability, who himself had to endure screams of 'spastic' from two aggressive men in the street just a fortnight ago. 'And it's getting worse. If we don't address low-level abuse, we let people think it's acceptable, allowing it to proliferate and become mainstream.'

An investigation into crime against the disabled revealed that nearly two-thirds of people with mental health problems had been abused in the street in the previous two years, with about a quarter suffering sexual harassment or physical assault. But only 141 disabled hate crimes were successfully prosecuted in a year, compared with 778 homophobic cases and 6,689 racial cases. The Home Office does not even bother collecting statistics on disability hate crime, unlike racially or religious-based offences.

We are retreating in the fight to offer respect and inclusion to more than one million of our fellow citizens. John Bangs, head of education at the National Union of Teachers, admitted to me that the promotion of disabled rights had fallen back in the past decade while schools concentrated on racism and homophobia. And as the struggle for inclusion in society gets harder, the stares get more pronounced, the insults more widely heard, the harassment worse – and more and more people with disabilities will abandon their personal battles and withdraw to their ghettos.

Is this really what we want? Or should we at the very least start to mind our language?

6 November 2009

Acceptable language for disability

Language is a highly contentious issue, and it's difficult to come up with a 'perfect' list of terminology that won't offend anyone. We recommend the following language as being least likely to cause offence, but its always worth checking locally as there are regional variations in preferred language:

⇨ someone without a disability – non-disabled person.

⇨ someone with a disability – disabled person.

⇨ person with a hearing impairment – D/deaf person, sign language user, partially hearing person, deafened person, hard of hearing person...

⇨ person with a visual impairment – blind person, partially sighted person, guide dog user.

⇨ people with a learning disability – learning disabled people, people with learning difficulties.

⇨ people with a mobility impairment – wheelchair users, mobility impaired person, person with a physical impairment – physically disabled person.

⇨ person with an impairment related to their mental health – person with mental health needs, person experiencing/with experience of mental distress, survivor.

⇨ person with a hidden impairment – person with a hidden disability, person who has..., person with experience of..., person with...

⇨ someone who works alongside a disabled person to meet their access needs or ensure their needs are met – personal assistant (PA), facilitator, support worker, carer, care worker, participation assistant, interpreter, communicator, notetaker, reader, educational aid, mobility guide...

⇨ The above information is reprinted with kind permission from Get a Plan. Visit www.getaplan.org. uk for more information.

THE INDEPENDENT / GET A PLAN

Unequal treatment

The NHS often helps to maintain or even spread disablist attitudes, says Andy Rickell.

If we intend to banish disablism, we must tackle the beliefs that keep it going. As disablism is a deep-seated issue, we have to challenge some powerful interests.

The ultimate origin of disablist behaviour and institutional disablism is disablist attitudes – the belief that people with impairments are second-class citizens, not fully human, and therefore not entitled to equal treatment with unimpaired people.

Two key propagators of these attitudes are our current health services and the media. This time, let's think about health services. The NHS: a very powerful interest indeed!

I believe that medical professionals genuinely seek to do their best, with dedication, skill, and a belief that they support people's human rights.

However, their operating environment at least perpetuates disablism, and may add to it.

The high level of medical understanding of the professional, and their role as gatekeeper to services, compared to the relative ignorance of the disabled person, creates a power imbalance in the relationship, which renders the disabled person unnecessarily dependent on the professional's judgement. This must be equalised, by supporting disabled people so that we know much more about our conditions and their management, and also by professionals listening to us as experts on our needs. Disabled people need 'choice and control' over our health and any medical interventions too.

Secondly, society requires major judgements by medical professionals in decisions on 'quality of life' – from providing life-saving treatment, to decisions about rationed resources, including equipment and therapy. Anecdotal evidence from disabled people suggests serious underestimation of quality of life for disabled people by professionals. This affects treatment decisions, and the negative attitudes that professionals impart to disabled people and their families. Medical professionals' training must include an understanding of the positive reality of disabled people's lives.

Thirdly, there is an emphasis on surgical and drug interventions rather than therapeutic ones, and a low priority given to supporting rapid rehabilitation. We need a model which meets the holistic health needs of the disabled person for getting on with their life rather than treating them as malfunctioning equipment that can be sidelined, and which also recognises the role that self-image, self-identity and self-esteem play in a disabled person's overall health.

Finally, there is the belief that medical advance is the ultimate answer to eradicating impairment, in the extreme reflected by the geneticist who said: 'One day, it will be a sin to have a disabled baby.' Not in my Bible. What is fascinating about this proposal is both the value judgement, which is superstitious and unbiblical, and its unscientific approach to impairment. Some impairment is indeed susceptible to ethical medical advance – great, let's encourage it. But some impairment is environmental, e.g. injury, emotional distress; some is due to human mortality, e.g. bodily wear and tear, and some can only be eradicated by destroying the person, e.g. genetic conditions.

To overturn these disablist attitudes, we need an NHS which positively and publicly champions the right to life in all its fullness for all citizens, and uses its power to educate the public in an understanding of health and well-being that acknowledges impairment as a normal part of a healthy society's communal life.

Andy Rickell is a former executive director at Scope

⇨ The above information is reprinted with kind permission from Disability Now. Visit www.disabilitynow.org.uk for more information.

© Disability Now 2007

Disability Living Allowance (DLA)

Disability Living Allowance – sometimes referred to as DLA – is a tax-free benefit for children and adults who need someone to help look after them, have walking difficulties or because they are physically or mentally disabled.

Who can get Disability Living Allowance?

You may get Disability Living Allowance if:

⇨ you have a physical disability (including a sensory disability, such as blindness) or mental disability (including learning disabilities), or both.

⇨ your disability is severe enough for you to need help caring for yourself or someone to supervise you, for your own or someone else's safety, or you have walking difficulties, or both.

⇨ you are under 65 when you claim.

Normally, you must have had these care or supervision needs or walking difficulties for at least three months and they are likely to continue for at least a further six months. However, if you are terminally ill, there are special rules for claiming the benefit.

If you are aged 65 or over, you may be able to get Attendance Allowance.

You can get Disability Living Allowance whether or not you work.

It isn't usually affected by any savings or income you may have.

Special rules – if you are terminally ill

If you have a progressive disease and you are not expected to live for more than another six months there are special rules for claiming to make sure you get your benefit more quickly and easily.

Medical examinations

You will not usually need a medical examination when you claim for Disability Living Allowance.

How much do you get?

Disability Living Allowance has two parts called 'components':

⇨ a care component – if you need help looking after yourself or supervision to keep you safe.

⇨ a mobility component – if you can't walk or find it very hard to walk, or you need help getting around.

Some people will be entitled to receive just one component; others may get both.

The care component and mobility component are paid at different rates depending on how your disability affects you.

How it's paid

Disability Living Allowance is normally paid directly into any account of your choice which accepts direct payment of benefits. this might be a bank, building society or other account provider.

You may be able to get someone else to collect your Disability Living Allowance if you wish. For help with this please contact your bank, building society or other account provider.

If you would like more information about how you can be paid by other means please contact the office dealing with your claim.

Effect on other benefits and entitlements

If you start to get Disability Living Allowance it might increase the amount of other benefits or credits you're entitled to, such as:

⇨ Income Support

⇨ Income-related Employment and Support Allowance

⇨ Income-based Jobseeker's Allowance

⇨ Pension Credit

⇨ Housing Benefit

⇨ Council Tax Benefit

⇨ Working Tax Credit

⇨ Child Tax Credit

Disability Living Allowance is normally ignored as income for working out these income-related benefits and credits.

⇨ The above information is reprinted with kind permission from Directgov. Visit www.direct.gov.uk for more information.

© Crown copyright

DIRECTGOV

The impact of Disability Living Allowance and Attendance Allowance

Findings from exploratory qualitative research.

By Anne Corden, Roy Sainsbury, Annie Irvine and Sue Clarke

Aims and objectives

The aims of the qualitative research reported here were to investigate the use and impact of Disability Living Allowance (DLA) and Attendance Allowance (AA), to increase understanding of the difference these benefits made to people's lives, and to contribute towards development of questions that might be used in further surveys.

Research methods

The study used the following methods:

⇨ Six group discussions with 24 professionals and advisers in touch with people who claim or might be entitled to DLA or AA.

⇨ Qualitative interviews with 15 adult DLA recipients, 15 AA recipients and 15 parents of child recipients of DLA.

⇨ A desk-based review of relevant survey instruments.

Group discussions were held in early 2009. The 24 people who took part in the discussion groups included Department for Work and Pensions (DWP) staff in the Benefits Enquiry Line, and Carer's Allowance office; staff in six local offices of PCDS; local authority staff from adult services in seven local authorities; staff working in advice agencies and people working in voluntary organisations. The study group of adult DLA and AA recipients and parents of children receiving DLA was purposively selected from a sample supplied by DWP of benefit recipients who lived in one of three locations (a city, an urban and a rural environment) in Great Britain. Fieldwork was conducted during the summer of 2009. The overall group included a range of people with different ages and personal circumstances, and a roughly equal gender balance. One-third of the adult DLA recipients were aged over 65 years. Interviews were recorded, and transcriptions used for thematic qualitative analysis.

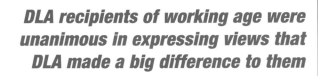

DLA recipients of working age were unanimous in expressing views that DLA made a big difference to them

Key findings

Information and advice about DLA and AA

There was a wide range of circumstances in which DWP staff and personnel in other statutory and voluntary services talk to people about DLA and AA. Advisers' experience was that general levels of knowledge about these benefits were low, and they spend considerable time correcting misunderstandings and wrongly based concerns. Advisers frequently discussed with potential applicants and their families what DLA or AA was for and how it might be used. The consensus among advisers was that, generally, DLA and AA had a major positive impact on recipients' lives. From their experience, they believed that DLA and AA benefited people by helping them:

⇨ maintain independence and control;

⇨ meet some of the extra costs of disability;

⇨ improve quality of life;

⇨ keep jobs or maintain contact with the labour market;

⇨ access other help and services (through 'passporting');

⇨ enhance physical and mental health;maintain warmer, cleaner, more comfortable homes;

⇨ relieve financial pressures.

Recipients' conceptualisation of DLA and AA

Adult recipients of DLA and AA perceived entitlement to be related to effects of long-term medical conditions and the need for help or care, or as a general boost to income for people with problems related to their condition. Parents also related entitlement to their child's medical condition and the additional expenses involved, and some saw wider purpose in enhancing family life, taking pressures off parents, and replacing lost earnings.

Using DLA and AA

Findings showed an important difference between the practical money management of DLA and AA benefits received, and the way in which recipients explained how the benefits enabled spending. The former was to do with the way bank accounts and post office accounts were used, how people made direct debits and standing orders to pay some bills, and which partner took responsibility for different parts of household budgeting. In addition, while some people separated out their DLA or AA (and sometimes other particular income streams) for particular purposes, others preferred a 'general pot' approach, thinking about the total money available to them, and paying for things as they were needed. Payment intervals for different pensions and benefits, including DLA or AA, the relative amounts received, and people's approaches to saving were all influential. When we turn from practical money management to thinking about how DLA or AA was being used to enable spending, findings show that DLA and AA paid to adult recipients enabled them to meet expenses of:

⇨ personal care;

⇨ transport;

⇨ food;

⇨ fuel;

⇨ home maintenance, including cleaning, gardening and small jobs;

⇨ health care, medical equipment and supplies;

⇨ telephones and computers;

⇨ social activities;

⇨ giving presents, gifts and 'treating'.

Findings showed that most direct personal care and support of elderly and disabled people living in the community was unpaid, and provided by partners, adult children and other family members. For many DLA and AA recipients, managing daily living also depended on finding solutions and working out ways of doing things which reduced the amount of direct help they needed, and enabled them to maintain control and some independence. Life was managed by being able to afford market prices for housework, laundry, garden maintenance, odd jobs and taxi rides; by buying frozen meals or buying hot meals outside the home; by relying on frequent use of telephones, and by running private vehicles. DLA and AA helped people to be able to afford these things. All parents of child recipients of DLA wanted opportunities to give their child the best possible life chances. They spent money on the particular equipment or activities that would help, and on treatment and tuition. Some parents had heavy expenditure on heating, electricity, transport and costs of maintaining or replacing appropriate clothes and shoes. Expenses spread across other family members, and into all areas of family life. Having DLA helped them pay for such items and services.

Other roles for DLA and AA

In addition to the way in which DLA and AA enabled people to afford what they needed, people attributed other roles to the benefits:

⇨ Helping practical money management.

⇨ Enabling access to other kinds of support (through 'passporting').

⇨ Providing a safety net, especially during financial transitions.

⇨ Preventing, or helping management of, debts.

⇨ Enabling people to live at home.

⇨ Keeping people part of society.

⇨ Acknowledging people's condition.

⇨ Enabling paid work.

What difference did recipients think was made by DLA or AA?

DLA recipients of working age were unanimous in expressing views that DLA made a big difference to them. All the adult DLA recipients in our study group were people who had been living on low out-of-work incomes for some time. Typical comments were that DLA 'enables me to live'. Some said, without DLA, they would not be able to pay their bills, or get the help they needed. Parents of child recipients who were living on low incomes said their children's lives would be adversely affected; for example, spending less on items needed for their disabled child, such as extra lessons. However, the more generally reported effect would be reduction in living standards for the whole family. Among DLA recipients over state retirement age and AA recipients

who engaged with the idea of what difference the benefit made most also used strong language. Some said it made the difference between poverty and a reasonable standard of living and without AA they could not afford the help they had, could not afford chiropody, or keep their home clean and warm.

Conclusions

Findings showed a wide range of ways in which DLA and AA are currently enabling elderly and disabled people to afford to pay for services and items they need. The benefits have preventive roles in helping people avoid moves into residential care or nursing homes, and maintaining or avoiding deterioration in health. Importantly, while DLA or AA often does not go directly towards paying for personal care, the benefits have a key role in reducing potential demand for formal services. This happens by enabling people to find their own solutions, both in the market place, and in accessing services from voluntary organisations, which are often not cost-free for users. DLA and AA recipients also believed that the gifts and 'treats' they were able to give to relatives and friends who gave practical care and help helped to maintain the channels of informal support within families and communities, on which they depended. For child recipients of DLA, parents were using the benefit in ways that will enhance their child's future life chance and opportunities. They were paying for tuition, physiotherapy, speech and language therapy, and equipment to encourage learning and stimulate response, all with a view to the future development of the child. In some families, DLA was being used in ways which support and strengthen family life.

Methodological findings

Our qualitative approach in interviews with DLA and AA recipients was to seek contextual information about effects of health circumstances and managing daily life, sources of income, money management, expenses and spending decisions. Embedded throughout this discussion were different opportunities to consider the contribution made by DLA or AA. We were able to explore the difference made by DLA or AA in a number of ways (through spontaneous comments; direct questions; prompts; exploration of advice received; exploration of perceived reasons for receipt; exploration of perceived relationship between DLA, AA and paid work; exploration of feelings about receipt; exploration of practical money management and response to hypothetical scenarios of loss and gain in income).

Conclusions from methodological findings

One of the principal aims of the research was to inform the possible development of quantitative research instruments for measuring the difference made by DLA and AA. The main relevant findings were:

⇨ Measuring impacts of DLA and AA does not require asking questions about the use of the benefits.

⇨ Process questions would provide a fuller understanding of the role of DLA and AA in people's lives.

⇨ There are significant differences between the needs and experiences of adult benefit recipients (of DLA and AA) and parents of child recipients of DLA.

The two main options are, therefore, to design a survey based on inputs and impacts only, or to design a survey that includes questions about how DLA and AA are perceived and used. The first option would not require constructing questions about DLA and AA while the latter option would definitely require a suite of questions that does not currently exist. It was outside the scope of this study to make any assessment or recommendations about whether any existing survey could in some way contribute to, or be used as the basis for, a survey of DLA and AA recipients.

However, scrutiny of relevant surveys suggests that none appears sufficient to measure the impacts of the benefits. A comprehensive understanding of the impacts of DLA and AA would, therefore, require a large dedicated survey instrument.

July 2010

⇨ The above information is an extract from the Department for Work and Pensions' report *The impact of Disability Allowance and Attendance Allowance: Findings from exploratory qualitative research*, and is reprinted with permission. Visit www.dwp.gov.uk for more.

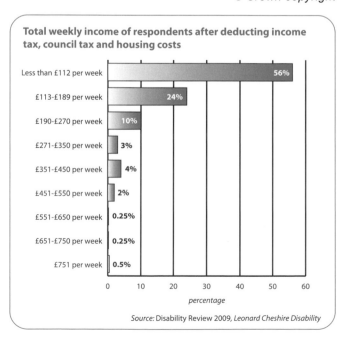

Total weekly income of respondents after deducting income tax, council tax and housing costs

Income	Percentage
Less than £112 per week	56%
£113-£189 per week	24%
£190-£270 per week	10%
£271-£350 per week	3%
£351-£450 per week	4%
£451-£550 per week	2%
£551-£650 per week	0.25%
£651-£750 per week	0.25%
£751 per week	0.5%

percentage

Source: Disability Review 2009, *Leonard Cheshire Disability*

DEPARTMENT FOR WORK AND PENSIONS

Poverty and disability links 'more pronounced'

Highest prevalence of childhood disability is found in poorest families, researchers at Warwick University found.

By Randeep Ramesh, Social Affairs Editor

Wealthy families in Britain are a third less likely to have a disabled child – a statistic that reveals an alarming social gradient because those families with such children are pushed further into poverty by the pressures of caring for them, according to new research.

Despite 15 years of legislation attempting to ease the burden on affected families, disability among UK children decreases with social standing. Now the highest prevalence of childhood disability is found in poorest families, academics at Warwick University found.

In the paper, published in the journal *BMC Pediatrics*, researchers found that households with a disabled child were £50 a week worse off than those without. This is despite the fact that the extra costs of bringing up a disabled child means families need an extra 18% in income. Nationally, this heavy burden weighs on the 950,000 families identified in the paper as having disabled children.

'We think the official [figures] underestimates the actual numbers by 250,000 ... and the huge inequalities that the paper clearly shows, that is of some concern,' said Clare Blackburn of Warwick University's school of health and social studies.

What is remarkable is the extent to which disability appears to be not simply just an accident of birth, she said, but a confluence of 'intergenerational poverty' and modern medical progress.

Blackburn said that the exact extent to which 'factors such as low income precede or follow disability is difficult to tell, but what we know is that poor diet and stressful living conditions do increase the chances of premature birth and low birth weight, which are indicators of future disability. Thanks to science, these babies live longer and medicine now keeps alive disabled children who may have died 10, 20 years ago.'

The Warwick researchers point out that debt was more common in those families with disabled children: the parents were unable to keep up with their council tax, water rates and telephone bills, and they were not likely to be able to afford basic items such as a family holiday once a year, a bicycle or even two pairs of shoes.

'It is a serious social gradient disabled families face,' said Blackburn. 'A disabled baby needs more nappies. Families' ability to work grows difficult, and finding childcare is a real burden. Households with disabled children will depend more on social security benefits and are faced with the additional financial costs associated with caring for a disabled child.'

Doctors said that Andrew Lomax's seven-year-old daughter Emily would not make it 'out of hospital' aged two weeks. Born healthy, she stopped breathing as a tiny baby. Those 20 minutes without oxygen had left her with a severe form of cerebral palsy. She was registered blind, unable to swallow, walk and breathe without an aspirator, so her two parents gave up their jobs to look after her and their two other children.

'Our income is £15,000 a year – about a third of what it was before,' said Andrew. 'It's all benefits, and I am a proud man who does not like to say it but family holidays come from the kindness of charities.'

Andrew says that he cannot afford to buy his elder son the Nintendo he craves. He is left scouring local papers for presents. His income is eaten up by fuel and petrol bills. 'We have to keep the house very warm for Emily, who is susceptible to pneumonia and the cost of running the specially designed car is prohibitive. It only does 18 miles per gallon. Most months we are hit by bank charges and missed payments. I try to juggle, but it is robbing Peter to pay Paul.'

Charities say that the disabled have lost out to other groups seen as more deserving – despite the disabled being in greatest need. Jonathan Welfare, chief executive of Elizabeth Finn Care, a poverty charity, said that the disabled have had their benefits cut while pensioners had been wooed with allowances.

'[By] denying the disabled the winter fuel allowance, the Government has left disabled people out in the cold. Disabled children living in poverty are often housebound due to the nature of their condition and for those with the most severe disabilities a warm home can truly be the difference between life and death.'

19 April 2010

⇨ This article was amended on Thursday 22 April 2010. The first paragraph of this article was amended to remove the word 'unlucky' in reference to families with disabled children. This was not in the reporter's original copy but was introduced when the sentence was reworded in the editing process. The *Guardian* apologises for any offence caused.

THE GUARDIAN

Barriers disabled children and young people face

Action for Children believes the Government's allocation of resources to disabled children should reflect the changes in the needs of these children.

Over the past ten years, the population of disabled children has significantly changed. This is because more children with complex and severe impairments are surviving due to medical advances, and there is a significant increase in the number of children diagnosed with autistic spectrum disorders. These increases contribute towards an increased demand for intensive support services, but in many cases local authorities cannot meet this demand. Eligibility criteria have also been raised and only children with the most complex needs now qualify for short-break support.

Our evidence is that a residential short-break service that started ten years ago will now be supporting disabled children with much greater levels of need. Many children require 1:1 support to stay safe and to maximise their social inclusion and personal development, and old budgets have been designed for just 2:1 support.

Local authorities seem to be struggling to increase funding and in many cases demand outstrips supply. The impact of true-cost recovery in the voluntary sector is adding to this. It is essential that services have sufficient funding to ensure their viability. With Aiming High funding, a transformation in the quality and sufficiency of short-break provision is anticipated in England. It is feared however that despite the announcement in 2008 by the Welsh Assembly Government the £21m for Wales, and the £34m earmarked for Scotland will not reach disabled children, as there are inadequate incentives for councils to prioritise the group, unlike in England, where authorities can be assessed against a performance indicator measuring parents' experiences of services and the extent to which provision meets core standards.

Universal housing, education, employment, leisure and support services must be made truly accessible to disabled children and young people

Inclusion

Universal housing, education, employment, leisure and support services must be made truly accessible to disabled children and young people.

We have run a number of consultation workshops for parents and young people to listen to their views. Evidence from these shows that parents want their disabled children to reach their potential and be able to participate in mainstream activities alongside other children of their own age. They spoke of wanting inclusive activities that whole families could enjoy together as well as activities that would develop their children's independence and individuality.

The need for reliable, consistent care from staff with the right training and experience was cited as being of paramount importance, as are flexible services that fit around the family's needs rather than those of the service provider. Action for Children supports the development of a creative, person-centred approach to ensure disabled children have the rights and freedoms afforded to their non-disabled peers.

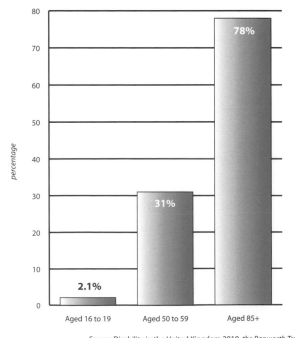

Disability is strongly related to age. This graph shows the percentage of people in each age group recorded as having a disability

Source: Disability in the United Kingdom 2010, *the Papworth Trust*

ACTION FOR CHILDREN

With housing, while we welcome the decision by the Government in England to reform the Disabled Facilities Grant (to help families of disabled children make vital adaptations to their home to cater for the needs of their disabled child), we are concerned at the speed of its implementation, given that it has been estimated that three out of four families with disabled children continue to live in unsuitable housing.

Play

Disabled children are seen as the group of children who cannot play yet ironically it can be this group of children who benefit the most from play. Play must be promoted for disabled children and young people.

A more inclusive approach needs to be taken to ensure that disabled children and young people have access to good quality play opportunities. It is essential that all those providing play opportunities to children have access to training, in particular about attitudes to disability and how to provide good quality inclusive provision.

Education

Education for disabled children and young people is as crucial to their developmental progress as it is for their peers.

While calling for more accessible universal services, Action for Children also recognises the essential role of specialist services. An example of this is schooling. We support the view that where appropriate and with support, the vast majority of disabled children could be educated in mainstream schools. In Scotland the Scottish Government have supported this view by implementing the Education (Additional Support for Learning) (Scotland) Act 2004 to support disabled children within mainstream or specialist schools. In England the *National Evaluation of the Children's Fund* (DfES, 2006) research brief on preventive services for disabled children showed that children attending both specialist and mainstream services demonstrated increases in confidence and abilities. Crucially, it must be recognised that parents, children and young people have the right to choose their education provision – a choice based upon sound information provided by all agencies involved, including prospective schools. For some young people a special school is more appropriate to meet their needs and these schools should not be seen as second best to mainstream schools.

Communication

It is essential that the Government recognises that communication is an essential component of social inclusion.

To enable all children and young people to make a positive contribution, they must have an effective means of communicating – and support to enable them to do so. Current provision is patchy. In order to improve the support available there must be a range of universal and specialist services. It has been estimated that ten per cent of school-age children experience speech, language and communication problems and one in 500 children suffers a severe communication impairment.

New technologies are key to disabled children communicating and participating in everyday life. For example, the Scottish Government needs to assist local authorities to provide services for disabled young people who are 16 years old and above through a transition period in order to access funds to assist them into appropriate education and training.

Action for Children is committed to helping disabled young people communicate through technology. The evaluation of our Warren Park Children's Centre shows how effective ICT is in preventing the social exclusion of disabled children, and therefore avoiding costly services later in their lives. We invite the Government to visit Warren Park and other similar projects.

⇨ The above information is reprinted with kind permission from Action for Children. Visit www.actionforchildren.org.uk for more information.

© Action for Children

ACTION FOR CHILDREN

Doctors say patients with a learning disability receive poorer care

Information from Mencap.

Almost half of doctors (46%) and a third of nurses (37%) say that people with a learning disability receive a poorer standard of healthcare than the rest of the population, according to a survey published today by learning disability charity Mencap to launch its new campaign, *Getting it right*.

The charity is launching the campaign as part of Learning Disability Week 2010 (21-27 June). Mencap's *Death by indifference* report in 2007 highlighted six cases of people with a learning disability who died unnecessarily in NHS hospitals. Since then the charity has received more accounts of tragic cases from families and carers. Mencap developed a charter with a number of the medical Royal Colleges which spells out the adjustments that healthcare professionals need to make to their working practices when treating someone with a learning disability. The charity now wants health trusts to sign up to its *Getting it right* charter to stop indifference and make these rights a reality for patients with a learning disability.

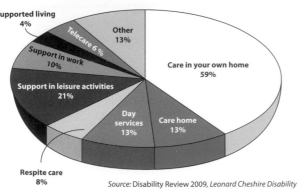

Funding of care packages for disabled people surveyed

A mixture of state funding and my own funds 26%

The state funds my care package, e.g. Social Services, Independent Living Fund 53%

I fund my own social care package 21%

Type of social care service utilised by disabled people surveyed

Supported living 4%

Telecare 6%

Other 13%

Support in work 10%

Care in your own home 59%

Support in leisure activities 21%

Day services 13%

Care home 13%

Respite care 8%

Source: Disability Review 2009, *Leonard Cheshire Disability*

The survey of over 1,000 healthcare professionals also found that:

⇨ almost half of doctors (45%) and a third of nurses (33%) also admitted that they had personally witnessed a patient with a learning disability being treated with neglect or a lack of dignity or receiving poor-quality care.

⇨ nearly four out of ten doctors (39%) and a third of nurses (34%) went as far as saying that people with a learning disability are discriminated against in the NHS.

By law, all healthcare professionals must ensure people with a learning disability have access to equal healthcare by making reasonable adjustments if necessary. But today's survey results also reveal that:

⇨ more than a third of health professionals (35%) have not been trained in how to make reasonable adjustments for patients with a learning disability, which can often mean the difference between life and death.

⇨ more than half of doctors (53%) and over two thirds of nurses (68%) said they needed specific guidelines on how care and treatment should be adjusted to meet the needs of those with a learning disability.

Almost half of doctors (45%) and a third of nurses (33%) also admitted that they had personally witnessed a patient with a learning disability being treated with neglect or a lack of dignity or receiving poor-quality care

Mark Goldring, Mencap's chief executive, said: 'Healthcare professionals have recognised they need more support to get it right when treating people with a learning disability. Mencap's *Getting it right* campaign sets out to ensure that ignorance and discrimination need never be the cause of death of someone with a learning disability.

'Our charter sets out a standard of practice and will make health trusts accountable to people with a learning disability, their families and carers. The fact that so many healthcare professionals recognise the gaps in their own training and the need for specific guidelines for treating people with a learning disability, shows the

need for urgent action before more people suffer. We want hospitals and health trusts to sign up today.'

Case study

Emma Kemp, 26, had a learning disability and was diagnosed with cancer. Her mother, Jane, was told that Emma had a 50% chance of survival with treatment, but the hospital staff were worried that it would be difficult to treat her because of her learning disability. Emma's doctors decided not to treat her, saying that she would not co-operate with treatment. Jane eventually agreed that palliative care would be appropriate.

Jane told Mencap about the discrimination Emma faced: 'Emma was a fun-loving young woman who loved her life and all of the people in it. She was denied her chance of life by doctors who discriminated against her. One doctor actually said: "if she was a normal young woman we would not hesitate to treat her". When I agreed that Emma should only receive palliative care treatment, I did so because I was then told that Emma only had a 10% chance of survival and that it would be cruel to treat her. I now know that this was not true, that I was misled into agreeing with the decision that cost my daughter her life.'

Everyone has a right to equal healthcare. Take action and help make it happen by signing up in support of the campaign at www.mencap.org.uk/gettingitright

About *Getting it right*

Getting it right is a campaign run by a group of organisations to improve healthcare for people with a learning disability. People with a learning disability experience poorer health and poorer healthcare than the general population. Mencap has worked in partnership with a number of organisations to produce a charter for healthcare professionals, to help them work towards better health, wellbeing and quality of life for people with a learning disability.

About Mencap

Mencap supports the 1.5 million people with a learning disability in the UK and their families and carers. Mencap fights to change laws and improve services and access to education, employment and leisure facilities, supporting thousands of people with a learning disability to live their lives the way they want. We are also the largest service provider of services, information and advice for people with a learning disability across England, Northern Ireland and Wales.

About learning disability

A learning disability is caused by the way the brain develops before, during or shortly after birth. It is always lifelong and affects someone's intellectual and social development. It used to be called mental handicap but this term is outdated and offensive. Learning disability is NOT a mental illness.

The term 'learning difficulty' is often incorrectly used interchangeably with 'learning disability'.

21 June 2010

⇨ The above information is reprinted with kind permission from Mencap. Visit their website at www.mencap.org.uk for more information on this and other related topics.

© *Mencap*

⇨ In some cases, even if medical aids or treatment are used to help control a disability, it is still regarded as a disability. Examples of this include the use of an artificial limb or medication to control epilepsy. (page 1)

⇨ In a review by the Leonard Cheshire Disability charity, 54% of respondents who had been disabled before completing their formal education had experienced discrimination or prejudice at school, college or university. (page 5)

⇨ All levels of learning disability are points on a spectrum, and there are no clear dividing lines between them. (page 7)

⇨ Autistic spectrum disorders are estimated to touch the lives of over 500,000 families throughout the UK. (page 8)

⇨ The British Dyslexia Association estimates that 4% of the UK population is severely dyslexic. (page 8)

⇨ The Disability Discrimination Act (DDA) creates rights for disabled people. Its main focus is on defining who is disabled (part one of the act), employment (part two of the act), access to goods and services (part three of the act) and education (part four of the act). (page 8)

⇨ Debenhams has become the first British high street retailer to break the taboo surrounding the use of disabled models in campaign photography. (page 10)

⇨ In England, disabled people are entitled to free bus travel at off-peak times on buses. In Wales and Scotland, disabled people and essential companions for disabled people are entitled to a free bus pass. (page 11)

⇨ In London, all newly-licensed taxis must be able to carry a wheelchair and all taxis must be wheelchair-accessible by 1 January 2012. (page 12)

⇨ The Government has a new initiative for disabled people on benefits – 'personalisation'. In a nutshell, it removes the local authority and in most cases, gives the money straight to the service user to spend as they see fit. (page 13)

⇨ 93% of families of disabled children in the UK are struggling financially. (page 19)

⇨ It is against the law to discriminate against disabled people in various areas of their lives: for example, at work and in the provision of goods and services. (page 20)

⇨ Service providers must make 'reasonable adjustments' to allow a disabled person to use their services. (page 21)

⇨ Two in five (40%) of disabled people surveyed by Ipsos MORI had experienced difficulties accessing goods and services in the last twelve months, with around a quarter of all disabled people (23%) directly identifying their experiences as discriminatory. (page 25)

⇨ An Ipsos MORI survey has shown that around a quarter (28%) of disabled people who had experienced difficulty in accessing goods and services had taken some sort of action to challenge this. (page 25)

⇨ An investigation into crime against disabled people revealed that nearly two-thirds of people with mental health problems had been abused in the street in the previous two years, with about a quarter suffering sexual harassment or physical assault. (page 29)

⇨ 56% of disabled people surveyed by Leonard Cheshire Disability had an income of less than £112 per week after tax and housing cost deductions. (page 34)

⇨ Wealthy families in Britain are a third less likely to have a disabled child. (page 35)

⇨ Almost half of doctors (46%) and a third of nurses (37%) say that people with a learning disability receive a poorer standard of healthcare than the rest of the population. (page 38)

Disability

The Disability Discrimination Act (1995) defines a disabled person as someone with 'a physical or mental impairment which has a substantial and long-term negative effect on [their] ability to carry out normal day-to-day activities.' The nature of the disability will determine the extent to which it impacts on an individual's daily life. The definition of disability includes both physical impairments, such as multiple sclerosis or blindness, and learning disabilities such as autism.

Disability discrimination

The act of showing someone less favourable treatment (discriminating against them) because they have a disability. This may be through outright abusive behaviour, or by denying them access to employment, education or goods and services. The Disability Discrimination Act (1995) states that it is illegal to discriminate against anybody because of a disability.

Disablism

A negative or prejudiced attitude towards disabled people.

Disability Living Allowance (DLA)

DLA is tax-free benefit provided by the Government to help people with disabilities meet the costs of day-to-day life. Some disabilities mean that it is difficult or impossible to stay in regular employment, and it may also be necessary to meet the high cost of specialist equipment and care. Disability Living Allowance is provided to help cover these costs.

Hidden disabilities

Not all disabilities are obvious. An individual who suffers from epilepsy, mental ill health or diabetes still faces the challenge of coping with a disability but is often not recognised as a disabled person, since to a casual observer they do not display the outward symptoms often associated with disability.

Learning disabilities

Learning disabilities, sometimes called learning disorders or difficulties (although these terms can have a wider definition and it would be incorrect to use them interchangeably with 'learning disability'), are defined by the World Health Organization as 'a state of arrested or incomplete development of mind'. Learning disabilities affect a person's ability to learn, communicate and carry out everyday tasks. Autism and Asperger's Syndrome are two examples of learning disabilities. People with Down's Syndrome will also have a learning disability. Learning disabilities were referred to as 'mental handicaps' in the past, but this definition is now considered obsolete and offensive.

Models of disability

There are two dominant 'models' or viewpoints of disability: the Medical Model and the Social Model. The Medical Model considers people in terms of what is wrong with them – their medical condition, their history and treatment. The Social Model makes a distinction between someone's medical condition and that person as an individual. It places the responsibility for disability on society, rather than on disabled people themselves. Disability is not viewed as a medical condition in this model, but is seen in terms of the stigma, oppression and stereotyping of a disabled person.

Personalisation

A Government scheme that allows disabled people to take control of their care by allowing the service user, rather than the local authority, to decide how the money for their care should be spent.

Paralympic Games

The Paralympic Games are a series of sporting competitions open to athletes with physical disabilities. They are held immediately following the Olympic Games. Athletes with disabilities including amputations, paralysis and blindness take part in a wide range of competitive sports. The next summer Paralympics will be held in London in 2012.

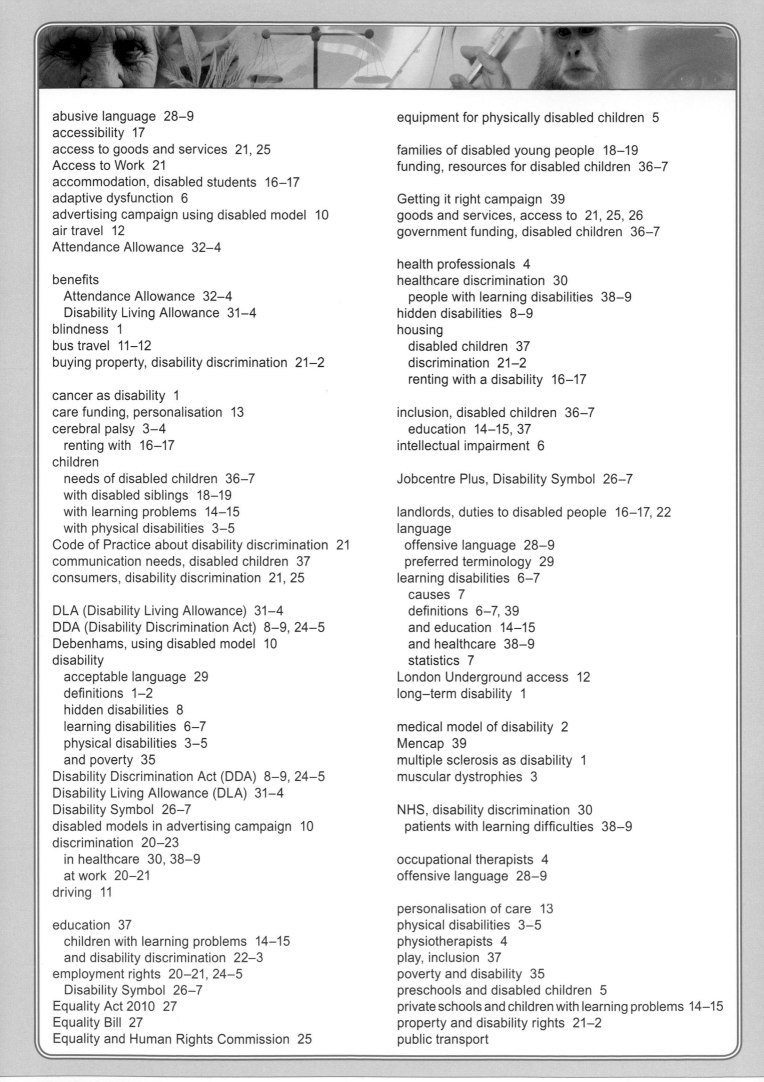

Additional Resources

Other Issues titles

If you are interested in researching further some of the issues raised in *Living with Disability,* you may like to read the following titles in the *Issues* series:

⇨ Vol. 198 *Sport and Society* (ISBN 978 1 86168 559 9)

⇨ Vol. 195 *Alternative Medicine* (ISBN 978 1 86168 560 5)

⇨ Vol. 187 *Health and the State* (ISBN 978 1 86168 528 5)

⇨ Vol. 183 *Work and Employment* (ISBN 978 1 86168 524 7)

⇨ Vol. 178 *Reproductive Ethics* (ISBN 978 1 86168 502 5)

⇨ Vol. 171 *Abortion – Rights and Ethics* (ISBN 978 1 86168 485 1)

⇨ Vol. 167 *Our Human Rights* (ISBN 978 1 86168 471 4)

⇨ Vol. 164 *The AIDS Crisis* (ISBN 978 1 86168 468 4)

⇨ Vol. 159 *An Ageing Population* (ISBN 978 1 86168 452 3)

⇨ Vol. 152 *Euthanasia and the Right to Die* (ISBN 978 1 86168 439 4)

⇨ Vol. 141 *Mental Health* (ISBN 978 1 86168 407 3)

⇨ Vol. 119 *Transport Trends* (ISBN 978 1 86168 352 6)

For a complete list of available *Issues* titles, please visit our website: www.independence.co.uk/shop

Useful organisations

You may find the websites of the following organisations useful for further research:

⇨ **Action for Children:** www.actionforchildren.org.uk

⇨ **British Institute of Learning Disabilities:** www.bild.org.uk

⇨ **Citizens Advice:** www.adviceguide.org.uk

⇨ **Department for Work and Pensions:** www.dwp.gov.uk

⇨ **Directgov:** www.direct.gov.uk

⇨ **Disability Now:** www.disabilitynow.org.uk

⇨ **Equality Challenge Unit:** www.ecu.ac.uk

⇨ **Get a Plan:** www.getaplan.org.uk

⇨ **Leonard Cheshire Disability:** www.lcdisability.org

⇨ **Mencap:** www.mencap.org.uk

⇨ **Sibs:** www.sibs.org.uk

⇨ **TheSite:** www.thesite.org

ACKNOWLEDGEMENTS

The publisher is grateful for permission to reproduce the following material.

While every care has been taken to trace and acknowledge copyright, the publisher tenders its apology for any accidental infringement or where copyright has proved untraceable. The publisher would be pleased to come to a suitable arrangement in any such case with the rightful owner.

Chapter One: Disability Issues

What is disability?, © Citizens Advice 2010, *The Medical and Social Models of Disability,* © Get a Plan, *Physical disability,* © Children, Youth and Women's Health Service, *Type of school attended, Discrimination at school, college or university [graphs],* © Leonard Cheshire Disability, *Learning disabilities,* © British Institute of Learning Disabilities, *Hidden disabilities,* © National Union of Students, *Debenhams first with disabled High Street model,* © Telegraph Media Group Limited 2010, *Planes, trains and wheelchairs,* © TheSite. org, *Problems with public transport [graphs],* © Leonard Cheshire Disability, *Giving me control of my care has been a revelation,* © Guardian News and Media Limited 2010, *Disability shouldn't leave children disfranchised,* © Telegraph Media Group Limited 2010, *Renting with a disability,* © TheSite.org, *Home ownership and living circumstances [graphs],* © Leonard Cheshire Disability, *Siblings of disabled young people,* © Sibs, *Statistics about carers [table],* © Carers UK.

Chapter Two: Rights and Discrimination

Disability discrimination, © Citizens Advice 2010, *Employment rights and the Disability Discrimination Act,* © Crown copyright is reproduces with the permission of Her Majesty's Stationery Office, *Disabled people's access to goods and services,* © Ipsos MORI, *Disability two ticks symbol,* © Waltham Forest Council 2010, *Equality Bill passed by Parliament,* © Equality Challenge Unit, *Mind your language,* © The Independent, *Acceptable language for disability,* © Get a Plan, *Unequal treatment,* © Disability Now, *Disability Living Allowance (DLA),* © Crown copyright is reproduced with the permission of Her Majesty's Stationery Office, *The impact of Disability Living Allowance and Attendance Allowance,* © Crown copyright is reproduced with the permission of Her Majesty's Stationery Office, *Total weekly income after deductions [graph],* © Leonard Cheshire Disability, *Poverty and disability links 'more pronounced',* © Guardian News and Media Limited 2010, *Barriers disabled children and young people face,* © Action for Children, *Disability by age [graph],* © Papworth Trust, *Doctors say patients with a learning disability receive poorer care,* © Mencap, *How should care packages be funded? [graphs],* © Leonard Cheshire Disability.

Illustrations

Pages 3, 26, 37, 39: Angelo Madrid; pages 11, 17, 28: Don Hatcher; pages 14, 20, 32: Simon Kneebone; pages 18, 30: Bev Aisbett.

Cover photography

Left: © Gabriel Doyle. Centre: © Craig Toron. Right: © Jeremy Keith.

Additional acknowledgements

Research by Shivonne Gates. Additional research and editorial by Carolyn Kirby on behalf of Independence.

And with thanks to the Independence team: Mary Chapman, Sandra Dennis and Jan Sunderland.

Lisa Firth
Cambridge
September, 2010